Penguin Education

Penguin Science of Behaviour
General Editor: B. M. Foss
Abnormal Psychology
Editor: M. Hamilton

Clinical Neuropsychology

Edgar Miller

Clinical Neuropsychology

Edgar Miller

Penguin Books

Penguin Books Ltd, Harmondsworth,
Middlesex, England
Penguin Books Inc, 7110 Ambassador Road,
Baltimore, Md 21207, USA
Penguin Books Australia Ltd,
Ringwood, Victoria, Australia

First published 1972

Made and printed in Great Britain by
Richard Clay (The Chaucer Press), Ltd,
Bungay, Suffolk
Set in Linotype Plantin

Penguin Science of Behaviour

This book is one in an ambitious project, the Penguin Science of Behaviour, which covers a very wide range of psychological inquiry. Many of the short 'unit' texts are on central teaching topics, while others deal with present theoretical and empirical work which the Editors consider to be important new contributions to psychology. We have kept in mind both the teaching divisions of psychology and also the needs of psychologists at work. For readers working with children, for example, some of the units in the field of Developmental Psychology deal with psychological techniques in testing children, other units deal with work on cognitive growth. For academic psychologists, there are units in well-established areas such as Cognitive Psychology, but also units which do not fall neatly under any one heading, or which are thought of as 'applied', but which nevertheless are highly relevant to psychology as a whole.

The project is published in short units for two main reasons. Firstly, a large range of short texts at inexpensive prices gives the teacher a flexibility in planning his course and recommending texts for it. Secondly, the pace at which important new work is published requires the project to be adaptable. Our plan allows a unit to be revised or a fresh unit to be added with maximum speed and miniminal cost to the reader.

Above all, for students, the different viewpoints of many authors, sometimes overlapping, sometimes in contradiction, and the range of topics Editors have selected, will reveal the complexity and diversity which exist beyond the necessarily conventional headings of an introductory course.

B.M.F.

Contents

Editorial Foreword

That the brain is the 'organ of the mind' has been known for two millenia, but detailed information is less than two hundred years old. Progress in this difficult subject will always be slow, but the last two decades have seen a tremendous advance in our understanding of the effects of damage to the brain. This is despite the fact that the 'experiments' of nature on the human brain can rarely, if ever, lead to clear information and the value of experiments on animals is always in doubt because of the fundamental difference between human and animal brains. This is not entirely because humans speak and animals don't. The principle of 'encephalization' signifies that as we move up the evolutionary scale, then functions of the brain previously subserved by lower 'centres' move upwards into the cortex. Of course, this principle is derived from the data obtained from experiments on animals and observations on the effects of injury and disease in man, but it epitomizes the difficulties.

This short book presents a careful review of modern work done in the fields of neuropsychology. It makes no attempt to cover the whole subject but limits itself to a number of main themes which are well studied in depth. As an introduction to the subject, it is invaluable to the junior student and, as the formidable list of references shows, it is a book which is well worth studying by the specialist. The author, who has contributed much to these researches himself, is eminently suited to write such a book, for he has a capacity for sound judgment and caution which is evident in his careful evaluation of the contradictory evidence. He not only helps the reader to find his way through the subject, but gives him confidence to continue his search. Dr Edgar Miller has produced a clear and straightforward introduction to clinical neuropsychology which is a pleasure to read.

M.H.

Preface

Until comparatively recently a large proportion of psychologists working in the clinical field would have lumped all 'brain-damaged' patients together as having a common type of behavioural disturbance. Just as no physician would normally consider it meaningful to describe a patient as having 'heart damage' or 'lung damage' because there are a large number of conditions with different consequences which affect these organs, it is equally meaningless to describe a patient as 'brain-damaged' unless this term is qualified in some way. The purpose of this text is to present an introduction to the psychological changes produced by one particular class of brain damage, that which is localized to one part or another of the brain.

The writing of a short introductory text inevitably presents problems of selection of material. I have largely concentrated on the effects of damage to the major cortical areas and within each area have tried to select a small number of problems which could be gone into in sufficient depth to give some flavour of current thinking and research. The selection of issues must be to some extent arbitrary and naturally tends to follow the bias of the author's interests but I have endeavoured not to leave any major point completely untouched.

An author is solely responsible for the views expressed under his name and rightly so, but it is also true that those around him play an important role in the formation of his ideas. I have been especially fortunate whilst writing this text to have come under the influence of friends and colleagues in the Department of Psychology, University of Hull, and the Combined Neurological Service, Hull Royal Infirmary. In this respect I am particularly indebted to Dr Marion Annett, Mr Norman Guthkelch and Dr Alberto Fernandez-Serrats (now at the Hospital General de Asturias, Oviedo, Spain).

1 Brain Damage and the Evaluation of its Effects

Anything which disrupts the working of the brain or damages its tissues is liable to produce changes in behaviour. The study of these changes, often now known as 'Neuropsychology', enriches our understanding of the mechanisms by which the brain controls behaviour as well as providing information of practical value in the diagnosis and treatment of brain damaged patients.

There are two complementary ways of looking at the effects of brain damage. We can concern ourselves with the disturbances which may occur in particular psychological functions, such as language, intelligence or memory, without much regard for the type and location of the damage involved. Alternatively we can concentrate more on the anatomical approach, i.e. given an injury to a particular part of the brain, what behavioural disturbances are likely to occur? The former approach has been predominant in a companion volume in this series *Brain Damage and the Mind* by Moyra Williams and the latter approach will be used in the present volume.

Although the logical distinction between the functional and anatomical approaches is quite clear it is often difficult in practice to fit particular investigations solely into one of them. One area that causes particular difficulty in this respect is the investigation of 'aphasia'. Some studies of aphasia can be fitted into an anatomical approach but, in general, aphasia is best covered by a functional approach. Since it is also the case that aphasia and its related disturbances have been discussed in some detail by Williams (1970), there will be no further specific description in this volume.

The principal concern will therefore be with experimental studies of behaviour in human subjects who have suffered localized damage to one part or another of the brain through injury, surgery and disease. The discussion will be extended by selective reference to studies of infra-human species (mainly non-human primates) with experimentally placed lesions. As the approach is basically an anatomical one a limited knowledge of neuroanatomy will have to be assumed, but this should not be beyond that otherwise attained by most undergraduate students of psychology. Figure 1 shows the location of most of the structures mentioned in this work.

Before getting down to the main problems of interest, we must first examine the factors which determine the effects of brain damage and some of the basic theoretical and methodological issues which are encountered in this field.

Factors influencing the effects of brain damage

There are two types and these have been summarized in Symonds' (1937) statement that 'the symptom picture depends not only on the kind of injury but upon the kind of brain'.

Nature of the injury

The three variables determining the nature of the injury are the location, cause and chronicity of the damage. The location of the damage is usually regarded as the most important but the other two variables have been shown to exert appreciable effects (e.g. Blakemore and Falconer, 1967; Reitan, 1964).

In human patients strokes form the most common cause of localized damage although psychologists interested in the effects of discrete lesions have tended to concentrate on other types of brain damage such as tumours or lesions produced by surgery. Surgery may be used to remove tumours or epileptic foci and to place lesions designed to relieve particular conditions. Examples of this latter type of operation are leucotomy, with its many variations, to relieve certain psychiatric conditions, and thalamotomy to relieve tremor and rigidity in Parkinson's disease. (Further comment on the types of lesions involved will be made whilst discussing the evidence on their behavioral effects.) In infra-human species the lesion can be

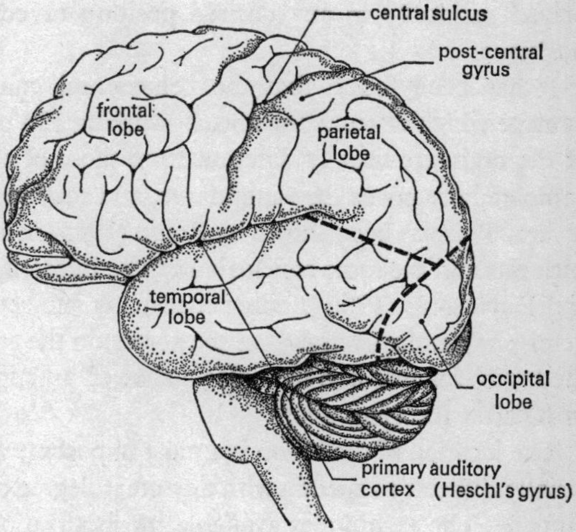

Figure 1a Lateral view of the brain

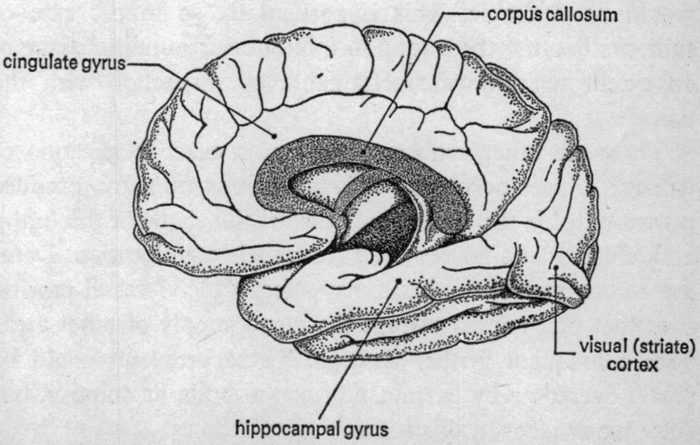

Figure 1b Medial view of the right cerebral hemisphere

placed surgically in any desired position or combination of positions.

It has been found that the behavioural consequences of damage which disrupts the normal working of a particular part of the brain are usually different from those of a lesion which completely removes the same tissue, and may indeed be more severe. This has been shown by Rollin (1955) in an experiment with rats and the same conclusion can be inferred from Griffith and Davidson's (1966) finding that many subjects undergoing hemispherectomy (removal of the cortex on the affected side of the brain) for infantile hemiplegia showed an appreciable gain in IQ after the operation.

The location of the lesion is a most important variable but is usually difficult to specify with any great degree of accuracy in humans. The techniques available for localization of damage, the EEG, various radiological procedures, etc., are only able to give an approximate locus. Even in cases which have been subjected to surgery, it is often impossible for the surgeon to specify either the anatomical extent of the disease process or the limits of removal of tissue with the sort of precision that would be desirable. This is particularly so in the case of tumours because these tend to infiltrate surrounding tissue to an extent not always ascertainable by inspection with the naked eye.

There are other problems preventing exact localization of damage. 'Space-occupying lesions' such as tumours, produce pressure inside the skull which distort the shape of the brain, and affect tissues far removed from their own location. Damage to one part of the brain may affect a blood vessel passing over that part and so disrupt the blood supply of other areas with consequent further damage. These problems could be partly overcome by examination of the brain at autopsy, but since many recover, this is rarely possible.

The localization of brain damage in humans is, therefore,

only approximate. By contrast, in work with animals the lesion can be carefully placed experimentally in an otherwise intact brain and the animal can be sacrificed at the end of the experiment with the exact site and extent of the lesion being verified by detailed histological examination.

State of the organism at the time of damage

Age is the most important variable here. In general, the younger the organism at the time of damage the less severe the behavioural consequences. This is particularly so in the case of children where such damage as would produce marked and prolonged aphasia in an adult may leave little evidence of any permanent speech deficit. Handedness is of significance, particularly where disturbances of speech are concerned (Subirana, 1958), personality factors may affect the subject's adaptation to deficit, and even sex differences have been claimed to affect the nature of temporal lobe deficits in man (Lansdell, 1961).

It follows from this discussion that the old idea held by many psychologists working in the clinical and abnormal fields, and unfortunately not yet entirely extinct, that all 'brain-damaged' patients can be lumped together in a single category, must be rejected. The effects of damage to the brain can vary very widely according to the nature of the damage and the state of the subject involved and can produce disturbances in every aspect of behaviour.

A basic theoretical issue

It has already been claimed that the locus of injury is an important variable. This prompts the question as to the extent to which it can be expected that psychological functions can be localized within the brain. There is, of course, no argument about the localization of basic sensory and motor functions within the brain since the areas subserving these are well established. The issue here is the extent to which the so-called 'higher cortical functions' can be localized. The controversy on this issue originated as early as the first half of the nineteenth century. The extreme positions put forward were on the one hand, the view that functions are strictly localized within the brain and, on the other, the notion that all functions depend upon the working of the brain as a whole (equipotentiality theory). As this controversy has been reviewed in detail by Meyer (1960) only very brief comments will be made here.

At the present time there is too large a body of evidence in favour of some degree of localization of functions for the theory of equipotentiality to hold, yet not enough for a viewpoint maintaining the strict localization of functions. A good example of this comes from the study of aphasia. For equipotentiality to hold, damage to all parts of the brain should produce language disturbance but, for the vast majority of cases, aphasia is only produced by damage to certain areas of the left hemisphere. However, within the rather extensive areas of the left hemisphere that can be implicated, evidence of strict localization of function is not very strong. Although there is some tendency for damage to particular parts of these areas to produce characteristic types of aphasic disturbances, e.g. more anterior lesions producing aphasias with a more prominent expressive component, these tendencies are not strong enough to enable the detailed localization of the various components that make up the very complex function of language.

Probably the most convincing evidence for the equipotentiality theory has come from Lashley (1929) with his theory of mass action. He defined mass action as a situation 'whereby the efficacy of performance of an entire complex function may be reduced in proportion to the extent of the brain injury within an area whose parts are not more specialized for one component than for another'. This theory was put forward as a result of studies of the effects of brain lesions on brightness-discrimination and maze learning in rats. It provoked a large amount of criticism and further investigation, some of which has failed to support the theory (e.g. Hunter, 1930; Pickett, 1952). In fact, although later writers have not always acknowledged this, Lashley's formulations were always much more tentative than their bald statement would suggest and he himself later accepted some degree of localization for certain functions (Lashley, 1933).

Neither of the two extreme views is acceptable and some kind of compromise solution is necessary. One such compromise is that of 'regional equipotentiality' (Meyer, 1960), in which it is held that whilst a behavioural function may be localized to a particular area of the brain yet, within that area, all parts contribute equally to maintaining that function. This compromise has some attraction but it does leave us with the necessity of specifying the areas subserving the different functions and with demonstrating that equipotentiality does hold within these areas.

Luria (1966) has provided an interesting treatment of the basic problem. Whilst the scope of the present discussion does not permit a detailed assessment of his contribution, it should be noted that he raises one point of importance that has often been ignored by others. Luria remarks that the term 'function' has been used in two quite distinct ways. On the one hand it may refer to the activity of a given small unit, e.g. the function of the rods and cones of the retina is to be selectively sensitive to light, and, on the other, to complex activities such as perception, memory and intelligence. In the first sense, 'functions' are, by definition, localized. In the second sense Luria prefers the term 'complex functional systems', which emphasizes the fact that complex activities of this type depend upon a whole series of functions of the former type. For example, visual perception depends upon the adequate functioning of the cells of the retina, the neurones forming the optic tracts, the striate cortex, etc., together with contributions from other functional systems such as memory. It must therefore follow that functions, in the sense of complex functional systems, cannot be strictly localized.

Problems of methodology and interpretation

It is worthwhile trying to clarify at the outset the methodological problems encountered in research with brain-damaged subjects. With animals the procedure is relatively straightforward. The animal can be used as his own control by testing both before and after the lesion is placed. By sacrificing the animal afterwards the exact locus and extent of the lesion can be determined. The provision of suitable control subjects either intact or with lesions elsewhere in the brain, is relatively easy. If considered necessary control animals can even be given sham operations identical with those given to experimental subjects but for the final step of making lesions in the brain.

With humans the situation is much more complicated. We have to rely on the 'experiments' performed by nature in the way of disease or accident, and so the subject usually becomes available for testing only after the damage has occurred. The subject cannot be used as his own control; he must be presumed intact in his pre-morbid state and his behaviour compared with normal controls which gives a much weaker form of experimental design. Occasionally, as in the case of patients undergoing psychosurgery or operations for the removal of epileptic foci, testing can be carried out before the lesion is placed. However, even these cases cannot be considered completely normal pre-operatively since there are the complicating factors of mental illness or the disturbance of neurological activity produced by the epileptic focus. In addition there is the increased difficulty of defining the anatomical extent of the lesion since the psychologist is rarely able to correlate his behavioural findings with a complete examination of the brain.

This comparison of the methodological problems involved in human and animal research emphasizes the potential importance of the comparative method in this field and, for this reason, a part of the discussion in the following pages will be concerned with research on animals, especially monkeys. Unfortunately this potential importance of animal studies for the understanding of problems in humans is somewhat attenuated by the fact that, even if verbal functions are excluded from consideration, it is often difficult to see much correspondence between the effects of a particular lesion in humans with those of a similar lesion in monkeys.

A further source of difficulty lies in interpreting the evidence provided by studying the effects of brain lesions. Of course, if we just observe and describe the alterations in behaviour which are associated with brain damage, no extra problems arise. The difficulty comes when we wish to make inferences about the functioning of the brain which is one of the most important uses of such evidence. The main logical problems involved will be outlined here; a more detailed discussion is provided by Weiskrantz (1968).

It is tempting to conclude that if by removing a particular part of the brain we can produce a deficit in behaviour, e.g. a difficulty in verbal learning following removal of the left temporal lobe in man, then that part of the brain must be responsible for the impaired function. As Gregory (1961) pointed out, this conclusion does not necessarily follow from the evidence as can be seen from the following analogy. If we were to remove the fuel tank from a car we would not be surprised to find that the car was incapable of moving itself forward. Nevertheless, it would be very misleading to infer that the function of the fuel tank is to propel the car. A similar situation holds with the brain and without further evidence, all we are completely justified in saying is that without this part of the brain the subject cannot carry out this particular function. It does not logically follow that the area involved *must* subserve this function. Other explanations are possible, and in some cases more likely, e.g. that all we have done is to cut an essential connection between two other parts of the brain.

Although Gregory, and other similarly minded critics, are correct in pointing out this logical difficulty in interpreting evidence, this kind of argument has sometimes been overconfidently assumed to deny the validity of ablation studies as a means of discovering how the brain functions in controlling behaviour. Provided we realize that in talking about the possible roles of particular parts of the brain, we are speaking of working hypotheses and not logically proven facts, lesion studies are, as we shall see, of considerable value in understanding brain functioning. Indeed, as Weiskrantz (1968) argues, some of Sherrington's most important discoveries on the integrative action of the nervous system were based on just that kind of inference which Gregory regards as invalidating experiments with brain-damaged subjects.

Another logical difficulty arises out of what might be described as attempting to prove the 'null' hypothesis. If we hypothesize that an area of the brain is involved with one particular function we thereby, either overtly or covertly, deny that it is involved in other functions and this is difficult to establish. An example may make the significance of this problem clearer. Monkeys with bilateral lesions in a particular part of the frontal lobes show what has come to be called the 'delayed response deficit'. This deficit will be described in greater detail later but, for the present, we can define it as an inability to make a correct response in a choice situation when the correct response has been signalled some time previously. The most obvious explanation for this would be that there is a memory deficit in these animals, but a large number of experiments using other types of task which involve memory have failed to give evidence of a memory deficit in frontal monkeys. This failure to find a memory disturbance under other conditions suggests that this part of the frontal lobes might not be involved in memory at all and that other explanations of the delayed response deficit must be invoked. Unfortunately, this conclusion is always open to dispute on the grounds that the deficit may still be basically one involving memory but that the other tests used either were not sensitive enough or that they did not involve the appropriate conditions for the manifestation of the frontal subject's memory defect. Such a line of argument is always logically tenable unless we can test under all possible conditions and with tests of infinite sensitivity.

This problem of trying to rule out a functional disturbance as a possible basis for a type of deficit is commonly encountered in neuropsychology and is difficult to resolve with confidence. However, one technique which allows us to rule out a possibility with greater, although not with complete certainty is that of 'double dissociation' (Teuber, 1955). In the example just cited, we could establish a double dissociation by showing that whilst frontal monkeys exhibit the delayed response deficit but not a memory deficit as assessed by other tests, subjects with another type of lesion perform normally on the delayed response task whilst showing a memory disturbance on other tasks. Establishing such a double dissociation would considerably strengthen our hands in ruling out the memory factor as a cause of the delayed response deficit because it demonstrates that the failure of the frontal monkeys to show a memory deficit on the other types of test was not due to the insensitivity of these other tests to memory disorders. This illustration also underlines the general usefulness of having control subjects with other types of brain lesions than the one of immediate interest.

Having discussed some of the most basic problems involved in research in this field, we can now go on to discuss the actual experimental findings in some detail. Since the majority of relevant investigations have been concerned with dysfunctions following damage to the major cortical regions of the brain it is therefore convenient to arrange the discussion under the headings provided by these regions. It will, of course, be realized that, in our present state of knowledge, such subdivisions tend to be arbitrary and that the regions involved must not be considered isolated from the rest of the brain. It must also be remembered that this volume will not attempt to give a detailed catalogue of all the behavioural disturbances found in brain-damaged subjects. We will concentrate on those aspects of behaviour that have led to systematic experimental investigation and many phenomena that have so far received only clinical description will be ignored. Those seeking full clinical descriptions are referred to the standard textbooks of neurology.

2 The Frontal Lobes

From a psychological viewpoint the frontal lobes have been the most enigmatic structures in the brain. They are particularly well developed in man, as compared with the other primates, and this has been one reason why some authorities in the past have claimed that the frontal lobes must be the seat of man's highest powers of reasoning or intelligence. Other early investigators were impressed by the fact that both monkey and man could lose large portions of their frontal lobes and yet show very little deficit in psychological functioning.

More recently, interest in the behavioural effects of frontal damage has been strongly influenced by two factors. These are the use of the operation of leucotomy for the relief of certain psychiatric disorders and the discovery of the frontal 'delayed response deficit' by Jacobsen (1936).

The notion that placing lesions in the frontal lobes might relieve certain psychiatric disorders was introduced by Moniz in 1936 and was taken up enthusiastically by Freeman and Watts (1942) whose operation 'the standard lobotomy' was extensively used for some time. This operation was quite radical and involved an almost complete severance of all white matter in the prefrontal region by bilateral lesions in the coronal plane. Because this operation turned out to have a number of unfortunate negative consequences it has dropped out of use and other more restricted operations have been devised. These operations include the removal of the grey matter of certain gyri in the frontal lobes (gyrectomy) and removal of the anterior portion of the cingular gyrus (cingulectomy). The most commonly used operations seem to be those which aim, by various methods, to section the fronto-thalamic tracts in the lower quadrant of the frontal lobes. Figure 2 illustrates some of the most commonly used surgical procedures.

Lesions of the frontal lobes and human behaviour

Much of the work has stemmed from the use of leucotomy as a psychiatric treatment, a major concern has been with its clinical significance. This has involved studying the effects of leucotomy on orectic functions. A further prominent line of interest has been in the effects of frontal lesions on intelligence. For various reasons these largely psychometric studies have not proved very enlightening but more recent experimental studies have added valuable information about the functional significance of the frontal lobes. This section will outline the results of psychometric studies of the effects of leucotomy on intelligence and personality and then discuss the much less numerous experimental studies in greater detail.

Intellectual functioning

There have been many studies which have looked at changes in intelligence-test performance as a result of various types of

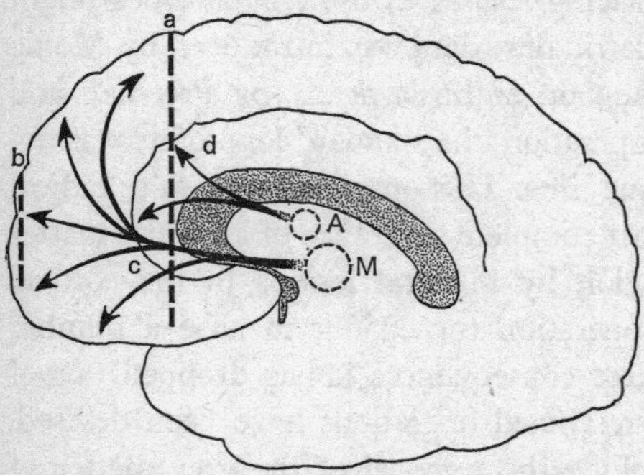

Figure 2 Psychosurgical operations
a Plane of section in standard lobotomy
b Approximate excision in topectomy
c Fibre tracts sectioned by a large number of modified psychosurgical procedures (e.g. orbital undercutting)
d Fibre tracts sectioned in cingulectomy
A Anterior nucleus of the thalamus
M Dorsomedial nucleus of the thalamus

psychosurgical procedure but, unfortunately, the results do not have a high level of consistency. Rylander (1951) has summarized investigations by himself as showing lowered IQs on the Binet scale as a result of standard lobectomy. He further claims that the follow-up investigation of his subjects showed this intellectual deficit to persist over a period of years although the exact length of the follow-up period is not given. Malmo (1948) reported a decline of intelligence as measured by the Wechsler–Bellevue scales following standard lobotomy or orbital gyrectomy. Unfortunately Malmo's post-operative testing was carried out between twenty-seven and eighty-three days after the operation and we do not know anything about the permanence of the deficit in his subjects.

Other investigators have either found no intellectual decline or a decline that appears to be only temporary. Hebb (1945) reported a single subject who showed no decline on the Wechsler–Bellevue scale following massive bilateral frontal removals (this was not a psychosurgery case). The second study of the Columbia–Greystone Associates (Mettler, 1952) found that, following a variety of psychosurgical procedures, there was a temporary decline on the Wechsler–Bellevue scale but that this had recovered when the subjects were retested about a year post-operatively.

In general, results suggesting that psychosurgery does not affect intelligence test scores have been reported at least as often as positive findings. When all the relevant studies, including many not cited here, are considered the inconsistencies are not easily resolved. The more radical surgical procedures, such as those employed on the patients used in Rylander's work, tend to give deficits that less radical procedures avoid. However, Hebb's case showed no deficit after massive bilateral lesions which were more extensive than those acquired by any case with a standard lobectomy. The interval between the operation and post-operative assessment is obviously important and too short an interval, as in the studies of Malmo (1948) and Petrie (1949a), may well lead to the reporting of deficits which are only transient in nature.

Apart from Rylander (1951), who does not give adequate details, the only long-term follow-up investigations appear to be those of Smith (1960 and 1964) and Hamlin (1970). Smith (1964) retested thirty-one (about 75 per cent) of the subjects used in the Columbia–Greystone projects over ten years post-operatively. Of these, about one third showed a decline in IQ despite the fact that they had recovered from an immediately post-operative deficit by the time the assessment at one year after the operation was made (Mettler, 1952). The older subjects seemed most susceptible to this long-term decline in IQ which also tended to be associated with the larger and more posterior lesions. Hamlin (1970) carried out a similar long-term reassessment of subjects from another major study of the effects of psychosurgery, the New York State Brain Project (Lewis *et al.* 1956). The follow-up interval here was fourteen years and it was found that intellectual decline occurred only in those patients who underwent upper-frontal-lobe surgery (superior topectomy). Subjects with lower-frontal-lobe surgery (orbital topectomy) had IQs similar to the unoperated controls.

There is a possible confounding variable in both these investigations. Since the subjects that Smith (1964) was able to retest were those that had remained in hospital, it could be argued that the long-term decline was not a necessary product of the operation, but that the general apathy produced by the more radical operations made the subjects more susceptible to the deleterious effects of prolonged institutionalization. Unfortunately, Hamlin (1970) does not state what proportion of his subjects were still institutionalized and whether there was a greater proportion amongst the group with upper frontal lobe surgery.

An original approach to the assessment of intellectual decline has been Halstead's (1947) quest for a 'biological' intelligence. Halstead used a battery of ten tests to measure this function and found that patients with frontal lobotomies were impaired on this battery as compared with controls. Patients with lesions in other parts of the brain did less well than the controls but not so badly as those with frontal lesions. It is difficult to assess the significance of this finding because the battery used to measure biological intelligence, is made up of a heterogeneous collection of tests of such functions as speed of finger oscillation, time estimation and flicker fusion threshold, which bear little relationship to one another and are far removed from the usual notions as to what is involved in intelligent behaviour.

A number of criticisms can be made of these studies of changes in intelligence-test scores. There are a number of methodological problems (such as ensuring a truly comparable control group that can be tested and retested over the same time intervals) which have not been adequately resolved in all the investigations cited. Even if the methodological problems can be considered to have been satisfactorily overcome, there is still a basic problem of interpretation. Most tests of general intelligence contain a wide range of different types of item which intercorrelate at a relatively low level but of which each correlate highly with a general factor of intelligence. This characteristic is true of the Wechsler and Binet scales used in the work discussed so far and is a sound general principle for measuring intelligence in normal subjects. Unfortunately, if a decline in an intelligence test score is demonstrated in an abnormal group, it is not clear without further analysis whether the deficit is due to a decline in the underlying general factor of the intelligence or to a decline in one or more of the specific functions involved in the sub-tests. For this reason looking at changes in IQ is not a very illuminating way of assessing the effects of any kind of brain damage.

A way of avoiding this criticism is to use tests of intellectual functioning which employ only a single type of test item. One such test often used in studies of psychosurgery is the Porteus maze. Porteus (1951) cites a number of studies showing a decline in mental age in this test following a variety of psychosurgical procedures. The results of Mettler (1952) and Petrie (1949b) confirm that a decline on the Porteus Maze test does occur but also indicate that subjects' scores are back to a preoperative level within a few months. Smith (1960), in another long-term follow-up study of subjects included in the investigations of Mettler (1952), observed that the decline on this test which had disappeared after about three months postoperatively, was again manifest after a lapse of eight years. Porteus (1951) regards these findings as showing that the subject after psychosurgery has a lack of foresight and an inability to plan ahead despite the fact that the test is usually regarded as one of intelligence.

Milner (1964) has studied patients undergoing operations to excise epileptic foci in the brain. One of the tests she used is the Word Fluency test from Thurstone's tests of Primary Mental Abilities which requires the subject to give as many words as he can beginning with a given letter within a set period of time. Subjects with left frontal lesions were found to be impaired in their ability to produce words as compared with subjects who had right frontal or left temporal lesions. Such a disturbance in verbal fluency following left frontal lesions is not surprising since many of the lesions in her subjects extended quite a long way posteriorly and came quite near to impinging upon an area which, in the left hemisphere, is associated with dysphasic disturbances (Broca's area in the inferior part of the third frontal convolution). Milner was able to demonstrate that the lack of verbal fluency cannot be attributed to an impairment of verbal memory by establishing a double dissociation between subjects with left frontal and left temporal lesions. The former had the disturbance in fluency and a normal performance on a test involving recall of previously learned verbal material, whilst those with left temporal lesions showed the reverse picture.

There is thus an appreciable body of evidence pointing to some degree of disturbance in general intelligence and other intellectual functions following damage to the frontal lobes. It can probably be assumed that the failure of many investigators to show any decline in intellectual abilities is due to the fact that these deficits are often not large and seem to be temporary in nature. The evidence provided by Smith (1960, 1964) and Hamlin (1970) that a further long-term decline in intellectual functioning may occur is of considerable interest. Further long-term studies are obviously required.

In reaching any conclusions it must be remembered that generalizations have been made about investigations involving many different kinds of lesion and that this assumes a degree of equipotentiality within the frontal lobes which may eventually prove to be unwarranted. Unfortunately the investigations necessary to clear up this problem have not been carried out, but the findings of Milner (1964) demonstrate that the right frontal lobe does not have identical functional characteristics to the left.

Personality

Since psychosurgery is usually performed with the aim of producing a change in the patient's personality, the question of personality change has produced a considerable amount of interest. A basic difficulty is that of measuring changes in personality due to the inadequacies of most of the available techniques. Because of this it is particularly important to have results which are cross-validated and little credence can be attached to isolated findings.

There has been only one group of investigations into the

effects of psychosurgery on personality which has given reasonably consistent results obtained from comparable techniques. These are the studies which have been carried out within the framework of Eysenck's theory of personality. The earlier studies used 'objective' tests (body sway suggestibility, perseveration, etc.) which have been found to correlate with Eysenck's factors of introversion–extraversion and neuroticism. The findings have consistently shown a decrease in neuroticism and an increase in extraversion following leucotomy in samples with largely neurotic subjects (Petrie, 1949a; Crown, 1953). Petrie (1949a) had tested her subjects three months after the operation but later showed that the changes found at three months remained equally marked at nine months post-operatively (Petrie 1949b). Crown (1952) examined a sample of psychotic subjects who underwent leucotomy and was unable to find any consistent change in either neuroticism or extraversion.

In a more recent investigation, Levinson and Meyer (1965) used the Maudsley Personality Inventory and the Taylor Manifest Anxiety Scale. Subjects were tested within a short time after leucotomy and tested again six to nine months later. Some of the subjects also underwent pre-operative testing. The results were similar to those of previous studies with a clear drop in neuroticism appearing at the first post-operative testing. A change towards increased extraversion did occur but developed more slowly than the change in neuroticism. These authors also looked at personality change in relation to clinical improvement. The patients who had the best clinical outcome tended to have a further decrease in neuroticism between the two post-operative testings whilst those with poor clinical outcomes tended to move back towards their pre-operative level of neuroticism. Those with the best clinical outcome were also more extraverted than the others.

Other investigations concerned with personality changes

have predominantly used projective techniques. An exception is Vidor (1951) who applied the Minnesota Multiphasic Personality Inventory to subjects before and after leucotomy. The most prominent change was a drop in the 'neurotic triad' which corresponds to the reduction in neuroticism found in the studies based on Eysenck's theory of personality.

The large number of studies using the Rorschach test raise in the sceptic the obvious questions of validity and difficulty of interpretation. For this reason they will only be cursorily surveyed. An exceptionally well controlled experiment was carried out by Allison and Allison (1954) who had eight psychotic subjects subjected to transorbital leucotomy and eight controls treated in an identical manner apart from the actual operation. They interpreted changes found on a number of Rorschach signs as showing a decrease in inner tension and self-awareness, and a loss of insight and enthusiasm. Their conclusions correlate well with the reported clinical impressions of psychiatrists on the changes in personality following leucotomy.

Another author whose interpretations of Rorschach changes agree with clinical impressions is Crown (1952). He found a decrease in the F score which was interpreted as indicating a diminution in tact and subtlety following the operation. In general, other studies with the Rorschach have either emerged with no definite findings, e.g., McFie *et al.* (1951), and the first Columbia–Greystone report (Mettler, 1949), or small changes which are inconsistent with the findings of other studies.

The personality changes due to psychosurgery have been well established in terms of Eysenck's theory of personality. There is a definite reduction in neuroticism and a less well marked change on the introversion–extraversion dimension in favour of increased extraversion. Levinson and Meyer's (1965) report indicates that changes on these dimensions are related to the clinical success of the operation. For those who argue that viewing human personality in terms of a very limited number of dimensions, as in Eysenck's theory, is too naive; there is little satisfactory objective evidence to go by. However, there aref airly well agreed clinical reports of the effects of leucotomy on personality and on the nature of the 'frontal' personality as found in patients who have had severe head injuries with contusion of the frontal lobes. These suggest that frontal damage produces a reduction in anxiety, lack of foresight, loss of social inhibition and social awareness, reduced insight and even a mild euphoria. The conclusions of some of the Rorschach studies are consistent with these impressions.

Memory and learning

Certain experimental observations, including the finding of the delayed response deficit in monkeys, have suggested that short term memory disturbances may occur following frontal injury. However, specific investigations into short-term memory in humans following frontal lobe damage have usually produced negative results. Milner (1964) found that patients with either right or left frontal ablations for the relief of epilepsy performed better than patients with left temporal lesions on a test of verbal memory. Ghent *et al.* (1962), had a large battery of tests of short-term memory involving both verbal and non-verbal material and utilizing the visual, auditory and kinaesthetic sense modalities. This battery was applied to groups of subjects with penetrating injuries of the brain and to non-brain-damaged controls. The results showed no evidence of memory disturbance in subjects with frontal damage as compared with either normal subjects or subjects with injuries to other parts of the brain. Positive findings of memory disturbances have been claimed, e.g. Kral and Durost (1953), but these are not convincing in view of the poor experimental methods and the lack of appropriate control groups.

Prisko (cited by Milner, 1964) used a modification of the

Konorski (1959) 'delayed-comparison' technique. In this type of experiment, two stimuli in the same sense modality are presented in succession (in Prisko's experiment the interval between the two stimulus presentations was sixty seconds) and the subject is asked to indicate whether the second stimulus is identical with the first. Subjects with ablations of the frontal cortex performed worse on this task than either normal controls or subjects with right or left temporal ablations when the stimuli were clicks, flashes of light or colours but not when the stimuli were nonsense figures. In interpreting these results Milner (1964) is of the opinion that they do not reflect a primary disturbance in memory. In the condition utilizing nonsense figures as the stimuli, the stimuli used on each trial were different from the stimuli used on any other trial. In the other conditions, where the deficit was found, only a small pool of stimuli was used and the stimuli used in each trial were sampled from this pool. It therefore happened that each stimulus was used several times over a series of trials. Milner hypothesises that the poor performance of the frontal subjects under these conditions was not due to poor memory but that this type of subject is unable to suppress the memory of previous stimuli and concentrate on the stimuli presented in the current trial. A similar explanation is also applicable to the experiment of Butters *et al.* (1970) in which subjects with right or left frontal damage were found to have mild impairments on a memory task which repeatedly utilized the same stimuli.

Despite the absence of any convincing evidence of short-term memory impairment, a number of interesting abnormalities in learning have been noted. Benton (1968) was concerned with the effect of bilateral as opposed to unilateral frontal pathology. He found that subjects with bilateral damage were impaired in the learning of verbal paired associates when compared with subjects having only right or left frontal damage.

Unfortunately this finding is open to serious question since Benton's bilaterally involved group had a high proportion of cases with 'degenerative disease'. It is improbable that any degeneration would be confined to the frontal lobes alone, even though it might be most prominent there, and it is likely that degeneration elsewhere in the brain would contribute to an impairment in learning.

Malmo (1942) had interpreted the results of an experiment on monkeys as showing 'an increased susceptibility to interference' following frontal insult. He followed this up by predicting that such increased interference would produce a more bowed serial position curve in the human learning of lists of nonsense syllables. Malmo and Amsel (1948) found this prediction to be upheld in cases of frontal gyrectomy tested after operation. In a further experiment (Malmo 1948) serial learning was tested both pre- and post-operatively on another five subjects. Four out of the five subjects took longer to learn post-operatively and this was due to a greater difficulty with the middle items in the list.

Differences in non-verbal learning have also been noted. Milner (1964) used the Wisconsin Card Sorting Test. This consists of a series of cards which have to be sorted into four piles such that the stimuli on the cards correspond to four sample cards. The stimuli on the cards consist of four different shapes (stars, triangles, crosses and circles) which may be in any one of four different colours. Each card has one to four of these shapes on it, e.g. two blue circles or three red crosses. The cards can thus be sorted by shape, colour or number. Testing proceeds by the subject placing each card in turn onto one of the four piles and with the experimenter saying 'right' or 'wrong' after each card has been placed. Initially the experimenter says 'right' when the subject sorts a card by shape although the subject is never told which is the correct dimension. As soon as the subject sorts ten consecutive cards by the correct dimension, the correct dimension is changed, say to colour, but without the subject being informed of this. When the subject has again reached the criterion of ten consecutive correct responses, the correct dimension is again changed. This procedure continues until the subject has reached the criterion for six dimensions (each of the three dimensions is used twice) or the pack of 128 cards is exhausted. Patients with dorsolateral frontal lesions were found to complete sorting by fewer dimensions than subjects with other kinds of brain lesions including those with orbito-frontal lesions. This suggests some differentiation of function with the frontal lobes. The poor performance of the dorsolateral frontal group was almost entirely due to a very large number of perseverative errors.

It seems that the subject with dorsolateral frontal lesions can learn to sort by the first dimension with normal, or near normal, facility. His difficulty is that when the correct dimension changes he continues to perseverate with the response appropriate to the previously correct dimension. The underlying deficit appears to be an enhanced difficulty in overcoming a previously established response set. It is interesting that Teuber *et al.* (1951) found little deficit in frontal subjects as compared with subjects with more posterior lesions when using the same test. Since Milner has found that the deficit she observed is only related to lesions in certain parts of the frontal lobes, it is possible that the subjects Teuber *et al.* used had different kinds of frontal lesions. Another, and more theoretically significant difference between the two experiments, is that in the case of Teuber *et al.* the correct dimension for sorting was shifted every ten trials irrespective of the subject's performance. It is likely that this procedure would not give the frontal subjects long enough to develop a strong response set to any dimension and thus disrupt learning to sort subsequent dimensions by perseveration.

Milner (1964) has also found impairments in maze learning in patients with frontal lesions. The subjects were required to learn a path through a maze formed from 100 nailheads set in a board in a 10 × 10 square pattern. The subject had to find his way from the bottom left hand corner to the top right hand corner along a given route by moving a stylus from one nail-head to the next. The subject was not shown the correct route which he had to find by trial and error. Errors were signalled by a click from the error recording mechanism. Patients with frontal lesions performed poorly on this task, as did those with right posterior and bilateral hippocampal lesions. The poor performance of the frontal group was related to an excessive tendency, not shown by other groups, to score errors by breaking the rules, e.g. by moving diagonally when only horizontal or vertical moves were permitted. The difficulty that the frontal group have on Milner's nailhead maze is reminiscent of the poor performance of leucotomized patients on the Porteus mazes. Milner attributes the poor performance of subjects with frontal lesions on both types of maze to an inability to inhibit inappropriate responses. A maze of any kind presents the subject with the response choices, to move right or left, or up or down, etc., and learning to make the correct responses involves inhibiting any initial impulses or response sets to move in other than the correct way.

Poppen *et al.* (1965) attempted to replicate with leucotomized schizophrenics an earlier investigation (Pribram, 1960) in which the subjects were frontally-operated rhesus monkeys. The apparatus consisted of a display of sixteen windows each of which could be lighted to show a range of different figures. Pressure on the correct window produced a reward. Initially, six windows were lit and the subject had to learn to press the one showing the correct figure. As soon as one correct response was learned according to criterion, another became rewarded and this went on until five out of the six possible stimuli had been learned in turn. Following this cycle of learning a seventh stimulus was introduced and rewarded. This cycle continued until each of the stimuli had again become the rewarded one. The testing procedure progressed in this way through several cycles.

A significantly smaller proportion of leucotomized schizophrenics completed the whole programme of testing within the given time than of a group of carefully matched schizophrenic controls. The operated human subjects, like the monkeys in the original version of the experiment, had difficulty in maintaining a strategy so as to reach criterion. The subjects in this experiment were similar to those tested by Milner on the Wisconsin Card Sorting Test, in that part of their difficulty in maintaining the correct strategy was due to perseverating with the previous correct response.

A number of abnormalities have thus been demonstrated in the performance of subjects with frontal lesions in experiments involving learning and memory. In many instances, careful analysis of the results has shown that the underlying deficit probably does not lie in the processes of learning or memory *per se*. The frontal subject seems to have difficulty in inhibiting any previously induced response sets and this interferes with the learnings of new responses.

Other experimental evidence

A number of other interesting experimental findings have been made but are difficult to classify under any single heading. Many of these have been reviewed by Luria (1966), Luria and Homskaya (1964) and Teuber (1964).

Both Teuber *et al.* (1949) and Luria (1966) have found disturbances in visual searching following frontal lesions. In the experiment by Teuber *et al.* (1949), a large array of simple visual stimuli (patterns, letters and numbers) was irregularly distributed over a large screen such that the total stimulus display covered a large part of the subjects' visual fields. Following a warning signal, a stimulus was presented in the centre of the display and the time taken for the subject to locate the identical stimulus in the rest of the display was noted. All types of brain-damaged subjects had higher search times but search times were especially elongated for frontally injured patients with unilateral lesions when the matching stimulus was located in the visual field contralateral to the frontal injury. Luria (1966) describes an experiment in which patients with frontal tumours and normal controls had their eye movements recorded whilst examining a picture. The scanning movements of the eyes of the control subjects were found to follow the main feature of the picture in a purposeful fashion whilst those of the frontal patients were chaotic and failed to follow the main features in such a systematic way.

Another experimental situation used by Teuber and his associates has been the Aubert Test. The basic situation is that the subject is sat in a chair in a darkened room and is required to set a tilted luminous line to the vertical. There are a number of variants to the task whereby conflicts between cues can be established. The subject can set the line to the vertical whilst sitting upright in the chair or with the chair tilted to left or right so that his head and body are also tilted. All brain-injured subjects performed normally with the chair vertical, but differed significantly from the normal controls when the chair was tilted. The normal tendency under such conditions is to over-compensate, e.g. if the subject is tilted to the left, he sets the line slightly tilted to the right. Groups with both anterior and posterior lesions exaggerated this compensatory error with body tilt but this was significantly more marked in the anterior group. A further experiment showed that the disturbance in the frontal subjects was not purely postural since such subjects had a normal facility to bring themselves back to a postural vertical whilst blindfolded after varying periods of tilt in the chair.

In a second type of cue conflict situation, the subject remains in the vertical position but the line to be set vertical is viewed against a background of oblique stripes. Under this condition, only the group with posterior lesions performed significantly worse than the normal controls. The disturbance in the performance of frontal subjects on the Aubert Test is manifest when there is a conflict between cues in different modalities, i.e. a visuospatial conflict. Conflict of cues within a single modality, in this case the visual modality, is not sufficient to produce an appreciable deficit.

Luria has described a large range of phenomena in patients with lesions of the frontal lobes and in particular has advanced the thesis that such patients show a disturbance in the regulative role of speech. Luria and Homskaya (1964) give a number of illustrations of this. The patient on being asked to squeeze a finger of the physician three times commences correctly but may continue with a series of uncontrolled presses after the three presses are complete. When asked to draw a circle the patient draws a circle but, instead of lifting his pencil from the paper as soon as the circle is complete, continues the line round and round the circle. On being asked to draw certain things, e.g. crosses, circles, squares in succession, the patient may draw the first two or three correctly and then perseverate with one of these responses, e.g. the circle, despite the fact that squares or crosses may have been requested. In these instances it is not the failure of the subject to remember the instruction that is at fault because the subject can often tell the examiner what the examiner's verbal instruction was, despite the fact that it has been executed incorrectly. Usually the subject gives no sign of being aware that his execution is at fault.

In all these instances, and many like them, Luria argues that the control exerted over motor behaviour by speech (Pavlov's second signalling system) is disrupted. It is particularly disrupted when this control has to be used to prevent some established activity from continuing or when this established activity has to be modified. It is when the circle is complete and the drawing movement has to be stopped, or the three presses accomplished and the physician's finger released, that the second signalling system is unable to reassert control over behaviour.

Lesions of the frontal lobes and behaviour in non-human primates

Delayed response deficit

As has already been mentioned, much of the work on animals stems from the classical experiments of Jacobsen and his associates (see Jacobsen, 1936). Jacobsen was the first investigator to report the 'delayed response deficit' in monkeys after bilateral frontal lesions. In his experiments, a large experimental cage was divided into two halves by an opaque screen with one half containing two food wells each covered by a cup. The screen contained a grille through which the subject in the other half of the cage could observe whilst one of the food wells was baited. The grille was then covered to obstruct the subject's view. After a set period a door in the screen was opened to allow the monkey access to the other half of the cage and his response noted. Subjects with bilateral frontal lesions were found unable to produce the correct response following delay as well as normal animals, although they were unimpaired when it came to learning a straightforward discrimination problem. There have been a very large number of experiments which have confirmed this delayed response deficit and no convincing negative findings.

A related disturbance in frontal monkeys is that of 'delayed alternation'. In a delayed alternation experiment the test situation is rather like that used in delayed response testing except that there is no observed baiting of one of the response alternatives. The two responses are each rewarded on alternate trials and there is an enforced delay between each response. There are a number of variations of this basic experiment (e.g. Mishkin and Pribram, 1955; Pribram and Mishkin, 1956) but animals with frontal lesions invariably perform badly. The delayed alternation and delayed response experiments are undoubtedly very similar. In both cases there is a cue as to which response will be correct, either by baiting in view of the subject or by the outcome of the previous response, and an enforced delay before the subject can respond.

It is evident from the review of Rosvold and Szwarcbart (1964) and the experimental work of Gross and Weiskrantz (1962) that there is a considerable amount of functional differentiation within the frontal cortex of the monkey. It is agreed that the area of maximum involvement in the delayed response deficit is the dorsolateral frontal cortex and, in particular, the region of the sulcus principalis. Lesions in other parts of the frontal lobe have a much reduced effect on this task. Lesions in other parts of the brain may also produce a similar delayed response deficit and Rosvold and Szwarcbart particularly implicate the head of the caudate nucleus.

Although the occurrence of the delayed response deficit cannot now be seriously disputed, its interpretation is still unclear. Jacobsen (1936) advanced the obvious explanation that the basis of the deficit lies in an abnormally rapid decay of recent memory traces but this theory is no longer tenable, at least without substantial elaboration. One difficulty with this explanation is that frontally injured animals have been shown to retain a learned discrimination at an even better level than normal controls (Weiskrantz, 1964). Such evidence as this strongly suggests that memory storage itself is not at fault but that there is some factor in the frontal animal which either prevents the normal laying down of memory traces or interferes with their recall.

Since the latter part of the nineteenth century it has been known that monkeys with lesions in the frontal lobes tend to be over-active. Gross (1963) investigated this phenomenon in some detail. His frontal animals had lesions in the areas especially associated with the delayed response deficit. As compared with the controls, they showed increased activity in the light but not in the dark. They also showed more activity when familiar auditory stimuli were presented and a greater decrease in activity after novel stimuli. This implies that frontal lesions produce hyperreactivity rather than hyperactivity.

Hyperreactivity could interfere with delayed response performance in a number of ways. It could cause the subject's attention to be distracted whilst cuing takes place or interfere with retention during the delay interval, e.g. by disrupting the use of the mnemonic devices like postural adjustments which might help to bridge the delay interval.

There is a certain amount of evidence consistent with this hypothesis. Wade (1947) has found that putting frontal monkeys under light Nembutal sedation improves their performance on the delayed response task. Malmo (1942) showed that if all lights were turned off during the delay interval then his frontal group did as well as the controls. If the animal fails to respond correctly because his hyperreactivity does not allow him to attend sufficiently well to the cue, then allowing the subject to obtain a reward from the correct receptacle before the delay period should help focus his attention on the correct response. Finan (1942) and others have found that this modification of the procedure does allow the frontal monkey to perform adequately.

Experiments like that of Finan imply that the frontal subject's main difficulty lies at the time the cue is given whilst that of Malmo (1942) implicates the delay period. One method of trying to establish the critical phase of the delayed response procedure is that of Stamm (1969). Stamm's subjects were allowed to respond with one hand and the ipsilateral prefrontal cortex ablated (this is not sufficient to produce a deficit on its own). Electrodes were placed in the sulcus principalis region of the other frontal lobe. It has been previously demonstrated that electrical stimulation of these electrodes would produce an effect analogous to a 'reversible' lesion. Electrical stimulation of two or four seconds duration was applied at various stages of the delayed response trial and it was found that the maximum disruption of performance occurred during the early part of the delay interval. Less severe disruption occurred with stimulation later in the delay period or during the last second of cue presentation.

Other investigators have concentrated on the response end of the situation. Here it is hypothesized that the frontal animal attends adequately to the cue and retains the necessary information but that something interferes with his production of the correct response.

One suggestion has been that the correct response is inhibited due to the perseveration of competing response tendencies. This theory has been elaborated by Mishkin (1964) who presents some confirmatory evidence. In one of his experiments, Mishkin presented the subject with a single food-well covered by an object. For five trials the subject was required to move the object and expose the food-well which was either baited or not baited on each trial. Following this preliminary training, the original stimulus was paired with a second object which also covered a food-well and conventional delayed response testing carried out. There were four possible conditions in the experiment. For two of these the reward pattern was consistent, i.e. if the object in the five pre-training trials covered a baited food-well then it continued to be the rewarded object for delayed response testing, and if the original object was not rewarded in pre-training then the other object was rewarded for delayed response testing. In a similar way the other two conditions involved inconsistent reward patterns with the original stimulus only being rewarded in delayed response testing if it had not been rewarded in pre-training, and *vice versa.* When the reward pattern was inconsistent, the frontal subjects performed at a normal level of the delayed response task but were impaired when the reward pattern was inconsistent. This result is in line with the notion that frontal monkeys do badly in the delayed response situation because they are unable to suppress competing response tendencies.

There has been a vast amount of work on the delayed response impairment and this discussion has merely drawn attention to certain trends within the literature. Grossman (1967) and the volume edited by Warren and Akert (1964) give more detailed surveys. As yet there is no single explanation that can cope with the whole range of findings that has emerged in the study of this phenomenon. The obvious explanation of a rapid decay in memory trace is inadequate and there is also evidence that the frontal monkey's performance might be disrupted at any part of the delayed response procedure, during cue presentation, the delay interval or at the point of production of the response. It may well be that we are not dealing with a single impairment but a task situation which shows up the combined effects of a number of impairments.

Other disturbances after frontal lesions

These will be just briefly listed. Deets *et al.* (1970), agree with earlier experiments in finding disturbances in social behaviour. There is also evidence that some frontal lesions impair performance in conditioned avoidance-learning (Waterhouse,

1957; Weiskrantz and Wilson, 1958), and this could be considered to reflect emotional changes. Disturbances in certain kinds of discrimination-learning have been noted. It is of interest that Gross and Weiskrantz (1962) were able to demonstrate a double dissociation between subjects with sulcus principalis lesions and those with lateral frontal lesions sparing the sulcus principalis. The latter group were impaired on auditory discrimination-learning but not in delayed response whilst the reverse was true of the group with sulcus principalis lesions. Among other things, this experiment suggests an appreciable degree of functional specialization within the monkey's frontal cortex.

Conclusions

The large variety of behavioural disturbances produced by frontal lesions makes it difficult to postulate a single factor underlying all dysfunction following frontal damage. Furthermore, the evidence, from both humans and animals, suggesting some degree of functional differentiation within the frontal lobes makes any unitary theory implausible.

One common theme that appears in the research conducted with human subjects in many different contexts is that of the perseveration of inappropriate response sets. Milner's subjects perseverated with a previously correct response on the Wisconsin Card Sorting Test and seemed unable to inhibit tendencies to respond in ways excluded by the instructions when doing the Maze test. Luria's patients persisted with a variety of responses after the required action was complete. Similarly, the frontal monkeys described by Mishkin have their delayed response performance disrupted when an antagonistic delayed response set has been previously induced. The establishment of response sets appears to be normal; the deficit lies in the frontal subject's inability to utilize feedback information from the testing situation which indicates that his established response is either wrong or needs to be modified.

A second point that emerges from this survey is that there is not a great deal of correspondence between the results obtained with human subjects and those obtained from animals. The delayed response deficit, which appears so predominantly in the animal literature, has not been satisfactorily reproduced in man. The closest finding with humans is Prisko's demonstration of an inability to match a stimulus presented at the end of a delay period with a stimulus given at the start of the delay. However, it would be wrong to overemphasize the dissimilarities. The perseveration of response sets in frontal monkeys already referred to has its correlate in human experimentation and the changes in conditioned avoidance response performance could be linked to the changes in emotional behaviour and neuroticism observed in humans. Poppen *et al.* (1965) have also achieved a replication of an experimental finding originally made on animals with human subjects (see p. 36). The general issue of the relationship between human and animal research will be taken up again in the final chapter.

3 The Temporal Lobes

A number of psychological dysfunctions following damage to the temporal lobes have been described by the clinical neurologist and the psychiatrist. Disturbances of memory and emotional behaviour are common following such lesions and may even occur in epileptics whose epilepsy can be traced to a small focus within the temporal lobes. Aphasic disturbances may occur, particularly with lesions in the more posterior parts of the temporal lobes. Finally, both auditory and visual perception have been found to be affected by temporal lobe damage. There are direct anatomical bases for perceptual disturbances since the primary auditory projection area (Heschl's gyrus) lies within the superior and mesial parts of the temporal lobes. Part of the optic radiation, that part known as 'Meyer's loop', passes within the temporal region and therefore lesions of the temporal lobe are liable to produce visual field defects in the contralateral homonymous fields. (A visual field defect is an area of impaired vision within the total visual field. Homonymous means that the defect is present in the corresponding parts of the visual field in both eyes.) Psychological investigations of temporal lobe dysfunction have largely concentrated on memory disturbances but interest has also spread to perceptual functions. The most commonly investigated subjects are those undergoing the removal of the anterior portions of the temporal lobes for the relief of epilepsy. This is despite the fact that such subjects are quite rare in general neurosurgical practice and temporal lesions of other aetiologies are relatively common. The most extensive studies of patients undergoing temporal lobe surgery for the relief of epilepsy have been carried out by Dr Brenda Milner and her associates at the Montreal Neurological Institute.

Of especial interest and theoretical significance has been the study of the few cases who have been subjected to bilateral temporal lobe surgery. This has been done either for psychosurgical purposes to relieve psychotic symptoms or to relieve epilepsy in a few cases with bilateral temporal lobe foci who have frequent uncontrolled seizures. Many of these subjects are remarkable for their severe and persistent amnesia and it is with the experimental study of this type of patient that we shall commence our survey of the effects of temporal lobe damage.

Bilateral temporal lobe damage in man

The most widely investigated and cited case is that of HM. Scoville and Milner (1957) first described this patient who underwent bilateral temporal-lobe surgery in 1953 at the age of twenty-seven years. The lesions involved the removal of tissue on the medial surface of both temporal lobes including the anterior two-thirds of the hippocampus, the uncus and the amygdala. The purpose of the operation was to relieve very frequent and severe epileptic seizures which were unrelieved by anticonvulsant medication.

HM, whose progress has been followed for a considerable length of time (Milner, 1966; Milner *et al.*, 1968) showed no decrement of intelligence after the operation. In fact his measured IQ has actually increased by thirteen IQ points to 117. This paradoxical finding is attributed to the cessation of fits. The outstanding change is in his memory. Immediately following the operation there was marked retrograde and anterograde amnesia. The retrograde amnesia (loss of memory for events preceding the operation) was quite severe but has gradually shrunk with time. Twelve years after the operation it largely manifested itself as some confusion about the temporal order of events occuring before the operation.

The severe anterograde amnesia (failure to remember events occurring after the operation) has persisted for at least fourteen years with little, if any, improvement. Many examples of the severity of HM's amnesia are given by Milner (1966). HM was unsure of his new address six years after the family had moved. He was unable to learn where constantly used objects, such as the lawnmower, were kept. HM would amuse himself by reading the same magazines and solving the same jigsaw puzzles over and over again without giving any evidence of having seen them before. This lack of ability to register information is almost total and leads to a lack of appreciation of the passage of time. When asked his age, HM will appreciably underestimate this in his answer. Occasionally information is retained. On one occasion in 1968 he was shown an American coin and was able to identify the head as being that of President Kennedy. On being questioned further he could recall that Kennedy had been assassinated. On the whole, this clinical picture of severe amnesic disturbance is characteristic of all cases of bilateral temporal lobe lesions where these are extensive or involve appreciable damage to the hippocampi. Smaller bilateral lesions sparing the hippocampi do not have the same drastic effect on memory (Scoville and Milner, 1957).

The particular importance of HM lies not in the extensive clinical reports extending over a long period after his operation, interesting and informative though they are, but in the detailed experimental investigations which have been carried out.

HM's verbal memory has been looked at in a number of ways. Testing digit span shows no reduction from pre-operative performance (Milner, 1959). Small pieces of information, like a three digit number, can be retained for several minutes providing that HM's attention is not distracted. As soon as his attention is claimed by something else, all recollection is lost. This can readily be explained in terms of the commonly accepted division of memory into a temporary short-term store and a more permanent long-term store. The normal digit span indicates that HM's short-term store is still intact but the severe anterograde amnesia implies that new material is not passing from short to long-term storage. HM is able to hold small amounts of verbal information in the short-term store almost indefinitely by constant rehearsal but, as soon as his attention is distracted, and the short-term store is required for other things, the material to be retained is lost irrevocably.

Wickelgren (1968) made a direct test of the hypothesis that the basis of HM's amnesia lies in a failure to transfer material between the short- and long-term stores. He presented HM with lists of items (single digit numbers, three digit numbers, and tones) at a standard rate. At the end of each list of stimuli a specially cued matching stimulus was given. The subject's task was to report whether the matching stimulus had appeared in the previous list. The closer the stimulus identical with the matching stimulus is to the end of the list the more readily it is correctly identified and thus it is possible to plot a decay function for items in short-term memory. The decay functions found for HM were within the range for normal subjects thus demonstrating that the short-term component of HM's memory is intact.

Results comparable to those found with verbal material have been found in studies of maze learning. Milner (1965) examined the performance of several groups of subjects on the same maze formed from a 10 × 10 array of nailheads as used in the study of frontal lesions. A small group of subjects with bilateral hippocampal lesions performed very badly. HM showed no learning in terms of decreased error scores but did show an improvement in time required for each trial. Corkin interpreted this as showing that HM was able to learn the proprioceptive skills involved in the task but not able to retain the correct sequence of turns.

HM's inability to learn paths through a maze has been shown to be dependent upon experimental conditions. Milner *et al.* (1968) studied his ability to learn shorter versions of both the nailhead and tactual mazes. When the mazes were drastically shortened it was found that HM could learn slowly, in terms of a decreased number of errors, and that he was able to show partial retention over a few days. This partial retention demonstrates that HM's inability to achieve long-term retention is not absolute. The authors argue that learning was possible on the shorter versions of the mazes because the mazes were then so short as to bring the sequence of turns within the subject's short-term memory span. This is an attractive hypothesis but there is no independent evidence of HM's short-term memory capacity for this type of information.

In contrast to his failure in the acquisition of verbal material and in learning paths through mazes, HM has shown an appreciable ability to learn motor tasks and to maintain his increased level of performance over time. Corkin (1968) found that HM's performance improved steadily over trials on both a pursuit rotor and a bimanual tracking task. When tested seven days after the last learning trial on the pursuit rotor there had been no diminution of performance over this period. Despite the good evidence of learning on these tasks, HM's learning curves were always below and parallel to those of the normal controls. Corkin has interpreted these results as showing HM to have a normal learning ability on these tasks. She argued that the lower performance level on the pursuit rotor and bimanual tracking is due to HM's slow reaction times. Since HM has been shown to have slow reaction times and reaction time is an important aspect of both the tasks used, this explanation seems satisfactory.

Other experiments conducted by Milner *et al.* (1968) have suggested that HM's performance on tests of visual perception and on the Wisconsin Card Sort Test is of a standard equal to that of the average normal subject or better. On a task devised by Gollin (1960) in which the subject is required to learn to recognize common objects from fragmented drawings, HM showed a normal level of ability on the task at the first trial and continued to show the same rate of improvement over successive trials, as control subjects. Retention was assessed by retesting after a delay of an hour but the degree of retention was not as great as that shown by the control group.

One important question that arises immediately is the extent to which the findings obtained with HM can be considered as typical of all subjects with similar lesions. Such limited evidence as is available suggests that HM's results can be regarded as typical although individual differences between subjects of a given type are always to be expected. The experiments reported by Corkin (1965) and Milner (1965) both used two other cases with bilateral medial temporal lobe lesions. These two subjects showed similar, severe disturbances in maze learning but their results were not quite as extreme as those given by HM.

Drachman and Arbit (1966) had five subjects with presumed bilateral lesions of the hippocampus and found results comparable to those obtained with HM. They first demonstrated that this small group of experimental subjects had a similar short-term memory span for both verbal and spatial material to a normal control group. The verbal material used was the conventional digit span test and the spatial material consisted of two parallel rows of lights. Pairs of lights were lit in sequence such that one light in the top row was paired with a light in the bottom row. In testing for recall, lights in the top row were lit in order and the subject had to respond by pressing the appropriate light in the bottom row. The short-term memory span was the number of pairs that could be correctly recalled at a signal presentation. For both types of material subjects were then required to learn to criterion with repeated trials, lists which were longer than the short-term memory span by a set number of items. The subjects with bilateral hippocampal lesions then proved to have greatly impaired learning of these supraspan lists. This result is readily explicable in the same terms as used for HM, i.e. a normal short-term memory capacity but an inability to transfer material to long-term storage.

It is worth noting that bilateral temporal lobe lesions have been occasionally used for the attempted relief of psychotic symptoms (see the review by Terzian, 1958) and for the relief of intractable pain (Gol and Faibish, 1967). It is not surprising that, in view of the severe and incapacitating nature of the resulting amnesic disturbances, bitemporal operations for such reasons have had little popularity.

Unilateral temporal lesions in man

The subjects most commonly used in psychological studies of unilateral temporal lesions have been patients subjected to anterior temporal lobectomy for the relief of epilepsy. Such cases are not very common but surgery for the relief of epilepsy tends to be carried out in a few specialized centres, the most famous of which being the Montreal Neurological Institute has facilitated their use as experimental subjects.

This class of patient is particularly useful for neuropsychological study because the lesion responsible for the epilepsy is usually very small and pre-operative assessments can thus be carried out on subjects who are as near to being neurologically intact as it is possible to get. Unfortunately their epilepsy is not their only disturbance and they do show mild disturbances in intelligence, memory and other forms of behaviour. Another difficulty with this group of patients which slightly complicates the interpretation of any findings is that some of the operated series have contained patients who were psychotic in addition to being epileptic. Because of the great preponderance of studies using patients operated on for the relief of epilepsy, the following discussion of experimental findings will only comment on the type of subject used if this is not the case.

In assessing the effects of unilateral temporal lesions it rapidly becomes obvious that the most important single factor is the side of the lesion. Many investigators in the past were unaware of the importance of laterality and this resulted either in contradictory findings or, since there is a tendency for left temporal lobe lesions to be encountered more frequently than right, the findings becoming an attenuated version of the effects of left-sided lesions (Meyer, 1960). For present purposes, consideration will generally be restricted to those investigations which have clearly distinguished left- from right-sided lesions.

Intellectual abilities

Clinically the most obvious finding after a left temporal lobectomy is that the patient is dysphasic. Usually the language difficulty is only transient and rapidly disappears (Falconer *et al.*, 1955). In view of this it is not surprising that there has been a consistent finding of a decline in verbal intelligence shortly after a left-sided operation. This has now been repeatedly demonstrated on the verbal scale of the Wechsler intelligence tests (e.g. Milner, 1958; Meyer, 1959). It seems probable that this decline is an exaggeration of a depression in verbal intelligence that existed pre-operatively in the patient with temporal lobe epilepsy. Slightly lower mean verbal intelligence levels have been found in such patients before operation by Meyer and Yates (1955) and Meyer and Jones (1957) on both the Weschler verbal scale and the Mill Hill Vocabulary Scale.

Changes in intelligence test scores in relation to right-sided lesions have been less marked. Both Meyer (1959) and Milner (1958) claim that the right-sided operation produces no change on the Wechsler scales. Milner (1958) had the largest series of subjects and, like Meyer, used the Wechsler–Bellevue Intelligence Scale Form I for pre-operative testing and then retesting with Form II after the operation. She claimed that, because Form II of the Wechsler–Bellevue is slightly harder than Form I, any practical effects due to previous testing could be ignored in examining the post-operative results. This assumption is unwarranted in view of Gerboth's (1950) demonstration of large practical gains when subjects are tested on Form II after having been previously exposed to Form I. For normal subjects, retesting with Form II gives an average gain of 11·1 IQ points on the performance scale. This gain of over two-thirds of a standard deviation is large when compared with a mean drop of 1·4 IQ points on the performance scale of Milner's right temporal lobe group. Milner's data must therefore be reinterpreted as showing a decline in performance IQ as a result of right temporal lobectomy. Blakemore and Falconer (1967) followed up eighty-six temporal lobectomy cases, some of which were in the groups studied by Meyer, and confirm that performance IQ is depressed after right-sided operations.

The changes mentioned so far have been those occurring within a few weeks after the operation. Both Meyer and Milner agree that the decline in verbal IQ following left temporal lobectomy has recovered after about a year post-operatively. Blakemore and Falconer find that the decline in performance IQ after right-sided lesions recovers within a similar length of time. Their follow-up period extends to over ten years in the case of some of their subjects and they have found no evidence of any further change in intelligence. Blakemore and Falconer's findings with regard to long-term changes conflict with those of a three year follow-up study conducted by Meier and French (1966). These latter authors found that performance IQs one year after a right-sided operation showed no decline as compared with pre-operative status but that there was a decline at three years post-operatively. This discrepancy can only be resolved by further long-term studies but it is possible that different results may occur in different centres using slightly different operative techniques and subject populations.

The effects of unilateral temporal lobectomy on intelligence seem reasonably clear-cut. There is a marked fall in verbal IQ following left-sided lesions which Milner (1958) attributes to the transient dysphasia following the operation. The decline in performance IQ following a right-sided operation is less marked but is nevertheless well established. These deficits on intelligence tests have generally disappeared a year after the operation. The only serious dispute concerns whether the right-sided cases then show a long-term decline in performance IQ.

The same criticisms of the usefulness of demonstrated changes in IQs as were made in Chapter Two with regard to the frontal lobes apply here also. In the case of the temporal lobes these are rather less potent, because the differentiation of effects established between left- and right-sided lesions does give some clue to the differentiation of function. From these studies it seems that the left temporal lobe is predominently involved with verbal functions and, since performance IQ is largely concerned with visuo-spatial ability, the right temporal lobe is likely to be implicated in visuo-spatial functioning.

Learning and memory

There is general agreement that verbal learning and/or memory is impaired by left temporal lobectomy. Again this seems to be an exaggeration of a deficit which is present to a slight degree pre-operatively. Both Milner (1958) and Meyer and Yates (1955) found that verbal learning/memory was poorer in left than in right-sided cases prior to operation.

Milner (1958) assessed her subjects on certain subtests of the Wechsler Memory Scale and concluded from this and other evidence that the impairment following left temporal lobectomy was in the acquisition of verbal material of any kind and irrespective of the modality of presentation. Meyer (1959) had a smaller series of cases than Milner but he investigated their learning capacity much more thoroughly. He had a series of paired-associate learning tests using both visually and auditorily presented verbal stimuli, visually presented non-verbal material (abstract designs) and even a tactile paired-associate learning test. In addition to varying the type of stimulus, Meyer also used both recall and recognition testing. The conclusions from this experiment were clear cut. There was no evidence of any learning impairment with right-sided lesions. Left-sided lesions produced the expected impairment in verbal learning but this was only for material presented through the auditory modality. The learning of verbal material in the visual modality was not significantly impaired. These results led Meyer to argue that the verbal learning deficit following left-sided lesions is modality specific.

Luria *et al.* (1967) made a detailed examination of two cases with left temporo-parietal lesions (these were not temporal lobe epileptics) and required their subjects to recall lists of verbal and non-verbal stimuli presented accoustically and non-accoustically. Like Meyer they found the impairment acquisition to be specific to verbal material in the auditory modality. On the other hand, Weingartner (1968) examined the serial learning of lists of verbal material in subjects after both left and right operations. He presented his stimuli visually on a memory drum but still found an impairment in verbal learning as a result of left-sided operation. This result supports Milner's thesis that the impairment is a general one for all verbal material. An explanation of these contradictory findings is offered by Blakemore and Falconer (1967). They comment on an as yet unpublished study by Blakemore in which the rate of presentation of material had to be learned through the visual modality was manipulated. This showed rate of presentation to be an important variable and that left-sided cases could learn verbal material through the visual modality if the rate of presentation was slow. With faster rates of presentation the deficit appears.

The only report of a long-term follow up of learning disturbances is that of Blakemore and Falconer (1967). They have followed cases for over ten years and report that the verbal learning deficit tends to persist for about three years and thereafter usually slowly recovers.

Investigations of other types of learning and memory have been made. These have either given negative results or shown up deficits associated with right-sided lesions. Stepien and Sierpinski (1960) examined short-term memory using the Konorski (1959) delayed-comparison technique. The stimuli used were tones or light flashes. Following the presentation of an initial stimulus there was a delay period, which may or may not have included a distracting stimulus, and then a second stimulus was presented. The subject was required to indicate whether the second stimulus was identical to the first and the delay periods varied between ten and twenty seconds. No subject with a unilateral lesion, whether temporal or in any other part of the brain, showed a deficit on this task. The only subject whose performance was impaired had a right temporal lesion with evidence from the EEG that there might well be another lesion in the other temporal lobe. Stepien and Sierpinski (1964) used the same experimental situation with other subjects, presenting evidence of bitemporal involvement (an epileptogenic lesion on one side producing discharge afterwards on the other) and found that these were also impaired.

Corkin (1965) and Milner (1965) have tested a large number of patients with various types of lesion, on the finger and nailboard mazes already described. Both investigators found impaired maze learning in subjects with right- as opposed to left-sided lesions. This finding was true of subjects with unilateral lesions in all parts of the brain including those with temporal lobe damage.

As in the case of the findings with intelligence tests there is a marked association between verbal impairments and left-sided lesions. Impairments in non-verbal learning occur with right-sided lesions but these are probably not specific to right temporal lobe lesions since similar disturbances in maze learning occur after lesions to other parts of the right hemisphere. On the whole, the impairments associated with right-sided lesions do not seem to be as clear cut as those associated with left temporal lobe lesions.

Perception

Perceptual disturbances in both auditory and visual modalities have been found. We shall first examine the evidence from studies of auditory perception.

Milner (1962) has reviewed the early auditory experiments carried out in Montreal by herself and a colleague, Dr Doreen Kimura. One of the first experiments was by Milner who gave the Seashore Test of Musical Talents to a series of cases who underwent unilateral temporal lobectomy to right or left hemispheres. This test, which is presented on a record, aims to take the subject through a number of basic musical abilities, e.g. discrimination of pitch, loudness, time and timbre, the discrimination of rhythmic patterns and a test of tonal memory. A number of changes were produced by the operations but many of these were not very large. The general pattern of results was for right temporal lobectomy to produce increased error scores. The types of discrimination most affected were those involving tonal patterns or judgements of tone quality. Surprisingly, these effects seemed independent of whether or not Heschl's gyrus was removed. According to some unpublished work cited by Milner, unilateral temporal lobectomy produces little or no change on standard audiometric testing.

At most there is a slight high tone loss in the ear contralateral to the lesion. The results of this experiment, and those of other auditory experiments yet to be discussed, cannot therefore be explained on the basis of a simple sensory loss.

Kimura (1961a) has used Broadbent's (1954) 'dichotic' listening technique. Pairs of digits are presented simultaneously, one to each ear. Usually a string of three pairs of digits is presented in this way and the subject is required to report the numbers he has heard. Normal subject respond by recalling the digits presented to one ear, usually the right first, followed by those presented to the other ear. The digits presented to the ear reported first are recalled *more accurately*. Pre-operatively, Kimura found this normal pattern of response held for both right and left temporal lobe epileptics but the total number of errors was greatest for the left-sided cases. The effect of the operation was to increase the total number of errors for the left-sided cases and to decrease the ability to report digits presented to the contralateral ear for both groups.

Kimura (1967) has evaluated the data from this and another experiment (Kimura, 1961b), together with data obtained from other experiments on normal subjects. She points out that a simultaneous dichotic presentation is needed to demonstrate these asymmetrical effects and that the sensory pathways from the ears are thought to project to both ipsilateral and contralateral hemispheres. She then offers the following explanation of her results. When, as in dichotic presentation, contradictory stimuli arrive at the auditory sensory region of any one hemisphere (one set of digits from the contralateral and one from the ipsilateral ear) then the contralateral pathway predominates and the message from the ipsilateral ear is inhibited. Hence the tendency for temporal lobectomy to affect the perceptions of digits presented to the contralateral ear. Since the left hemisphere is associated with verbal functions, a left-sided lesion will result in a greater diminution in the total number of digits recalled than the right. It also accounts for the fact that in normal subjects and in temporal lobectomy cases pre-operatively, digits presented to the right ear are better recalled than those presented to the left.

Further auditory experiments have been carried out. Shankweiler (1966) reports that the perception of melodies was impaired only after right temporal lobectomy. This result is consistent with Milner's findings with the Seashore test. Oxbury and Oxbury (1969) carried out a dichotic listening experiment similar to that of Kimura (1961a). They were particularly concerned with two points. Firstly, whether or not the operation involved the removal of the transverse gyrus of Heschl, and, secondly, the order of report. Since digits presented to the ear which is reported second tend to be reported less accurately, then the increase in errors from digits presented to the ear contralateral to the operation reported by Kimura could be confounded by changes in the order of report. Oxbury and Oxbury found that following right temporal lobectomy including Heschl's gyrus, there was an increased tendency for right ear digits to be reported first and this was sufficient to account for the change in error rate. Left temporal lobectomy produced an altered order of report, left ear digits being reported first instead of right when Heschl's gyrus was spared. When Heschl's gyrus was excised, the tendency to change the order of report was less marked than for when this gyrus was spared, but there was an increased error rate for right ear digits.

The pattern of disturbance in auditory perception again follows the general rule that verbal functions (the perception of digits) are most affected by left-sided lesions and non-verbal functions (perception of melodies and tone quality) by right-sided lesions. Although the differences described have been reliably established the magnitude of the effects is very small and often, specialized techniques, like dichotic listening, are required to show up any effect at all.

Following unilateral temporal lobectomy for the relief of epilepsy, the occurrence of visual field defects in the contralateral homonymous fields is common and changes in visual perception are therefore to be expected. The visual field loss is often that of the upper quadrant, but, according to Falconer and Wilson (1958), may range from being very slight to even a complete hemianopia (loss of a complete half-field). A more complete account of visual field defects and their corresponding perceptual anomalies will be found in Chapter Four.

Milner (1958) describes the performance of temporal lobectomy cases on the McGill Picture Anomalies Test. This test presents the subject with pictures of common scenes in which there is an anomalous feature that the subject is required to point out, e.g. a picture of a lion in its cage at the zoo shows an umbrella leaning against the inner wall of the cage. Subjects with right temporal lobe lesions were significantly impaired on this task in terms of both number of errors and speed of response as compared with all other tested groups, including left temporal lobectomy cases.

Other experiments have used the tachistoscopic presentation of visual stimuli. Kimura (1963) used various types of stimuli, letters, familiar and unfamiliar figures, groups of dots, and found that removal of the right temporal lobe impaired perception of unfamiliar visual stimuli ('nonsense shapes') but the left temporal lobectomy subjects were impaired in the perception of familiar material. The key feature here could well be that familiar material, like pictures of common objects, are readily verbalized and are normally most easily processed by their verbal descriptions. Thus this experiment again reflects the association between the left temporal lobe and the verbal functioning.

In a similar type of experiment, Dorff *et al.* (1965) presented stimuli to left, right or both visual fields. The stimuli consisted of pictures of common objects or letters. Both right-

and left-operated cases were found to be impaired in the perception of stimuli presented to both visual fields but the impairment was always greater in the contralateral field. When two groups of letters were presented simultaneously, one group to each of the two visual fields, the left temporal group were found to be impaired in only the contralateral (right) field whereas the right-sided cases were impaired in both fields.

Goldman *et al.* (1968) have shown that visual disturbances following temporal lobectomy apply not only to the complex perceptual functions but also to more basic sensory processes. They found that in cases without demonstrable field defects post-operatively, the critical flicker-fusion threshold was raised in left but not right-sided cases. Both left and right cases with visual field defects after operation showed raised thresholds even in those parts of the visual field that were not partially affected by other methods of testing.

In addition to the usual relationship between left-sided lesions and impairment in functions involving the processing of verbal information, these experiments on visual perception reveal other interesting differences between right- and left-sided lesions. The experiment of Dorff *et al.* (1965) points to the right temporal lobe having a greater involvement in visual perception since, under the condition of simultaneous presentation of stimuli to both fields, only right-sided lesions affected perception to both ipsilateral and contralateral fields. On the other hand, the experiment of Goldman *et al.* (1968) shows left temporal lesions to be more closely related to disturbances in critical flicker-fusion thresholds.

Sexual behaviour

The effects of temporal lobectomy on sexual behaviour have been explored by a number of investigators. Terzian (1958) in his review found a number of reports of hyper-sexuality post-operatively. The more recent studies of Blumer and Walker

(1967) and Taylor (1969) suggest that temporal lobe epileptics probably tend to be hyposexual. After temporal lobectomy there is an improvement in the sexual behaviour of a number of subjects and this improvement is correlated with the success of the operation in reducing seizures.

Hierons and Saunders (1966) examined a small sample of male subjects with various kinds of temporal lobe lesion (tumours, trauma, temporal lobe epilepsy, etc.) who were hyposexual. They felt that these subjects had a normal libido and that their sexual problem was in gaining and maintaining an erection. This contradicts Taylor (1969) whose study of a group of 100 temporal lobe epileptics resulted in the conclusion that the most common disorder was low sex drive, not in failure of ejaculation or the maintenance of erection. Taylor also noted that there was an increased frequency of sexual perversions in his sample.

Sex differences in the effects of temporal lobectomy. Lansdell (1961 and 1962) has suggested that sex differences may occur in the effects of temporal lobe lesions. His first report was a study of fifty-five subjects with various neurological lesions using the Gorham Proverbs Test. He found that, in the case of temporal lobe lesions, the ability to explain proverbs was impaired following left-sided lesions in males only. Since no statistical analysis is recorded and the number of temporal lobe subjects was small, little credence can be attached to this as an isolated finding. However, in his later paper (Lansdell, 1962) he used the Graves Design Judgement Test (this requires the subject to select the most aesthetically satisfying design from pairs of abstract designs) and found that performance was impaired for the males after right temporal lobectomy and after left-sided operations in females. These differences were highly significant statistically.

These results are the only ones known to the writer which

suggest that the organization of functioning within the brain may be dependent on sex. It is difficult to accept this and further investigation of this problem is obviously necessary. Lansdell points out that females have been shown to have a positive correlation between level of artistic interest and verbal reasoning whilst males do not. This could be used as an explanation of Lansdell's (1962) finding but really only pushes the problem one stage further back to explaining why this correlation should exist in females but not in males.

The effect of temporal lobe lesions in animals

The classic experiments with monkeys were those reported in the 1930s by Kluver and Bucy and which involved the bilateral removal of large parts of the temporal lobes. The behavioural effects of such lesions are well documented and are commonly referred to as the 'Kluver-Bucy syndrome'. The main features of this syndrome have been conveniently summarized by Kluver (1958). There is a visual agnosia in which the animal appears not to understand the significance of visual stimuli despite an intact visual sensory system and a tendency to examine objects by placing them in the mouth. Attention is disturbed, with a tendency to take note of every visual stimulus. There is a diminution in emotional responsiveness, an increase in sexual behaviour and often a change in dietary habits.

More recent research on temporal lobe functions in animals has used more restricted lesions aimed at specific structures within the temporal lobes like the hippocampal formation. The literature on this is vast, and, as with the case of frontal lesions in animals, it will only be possible to discuss general trends and describe a few illustrative experiments. In particular we shall concentrate on the effects of hippocampal and inferotemporal lesions.

Hippocampal lesions

The most widely reported disturbances following hippocampal lesions are in the learning of visual discriminations, e.g. Mishkin (1954), and Orbach *et al.* (1960). Cordeau and Mahut (1964) also found that monkeys with medial temporal lesions involving the hippocampal formation were impaired on visual discrimination-learning but that their subjects were able to learn such discriminations with normal facility two years after the operation.

This disturbance in visual discrimination-learning has been found with both simultaneous and successive discrimination tasks. In simultaneous discrimination-learning, e.g. Mishkin (1954), the subject is presented with two different stimuli on each trial and has to learn to respond to one of these. Successive discrimination tasks, e.g. Cordeau and Mahut (1964), present the subject with only one of the two critical stimuli on each trial. The subject then has to learn to respond one way for one of the stimuli and another way when the other stimulus is presented. An experiment with hippocampectomized rats by Kimble (1963) failed to support the findings obtained with monkeys in that his rats were impaired on successive, but not simultaneous, discrimination-learning. This discrepancy might be resolved in terms of task difficulty since Kimble used a very simple discrimination (black from white) and successive discriminations are harder to learn than simultaneous ones. Thus all visual discrimination-learning might be impaired if the task is hard enough.

Difficulties in learning sensory discriminations in other modalities have been reported by some authors. Orbach *et al.* (1960) found a mild retardation in relearning a tactile size discrimination that had been acquired pre-operatively. Cordeau and Mahut (1964) have claimed that disturbances also occur with auditory discrimination tasks. There is some contradictory evidence in the case of the auditory modality (Weiskrantz *et al.* (1962), but it does seem that the deficit in discrimination-learning is not confined to the visual modality alone.

In addition to impairing discrimination-learning after the lesions have been made, hippocampal removals may also disrupt and retention of discriminations learned pre-operatively. Correll and Scoville (1965) found this to be the case for the more difficult visual discrimination tasks. These same authors found that once discrimination-learning had occurred in subjects with hippocampal lesions, then the discrimination is retained normally.

Disturbances on other types of task have been reported. Orbach *et al.* (1960), examined the performance of their monkeys on delayed response and delayed alternation performance. They found that hippocampectomy affected delayed alternation but not delayed response performance. This finding is consistent with that of Mishkin (1954) who found that monkeys trained on a delayed response task pre-operatively showed no decrement post-operatively. In view of the following theoretical discussion it is of interest that animals with hippocampal lesions have great difficulty in learning passive avoidance tasks where the subject has to learn to inhibit an established response in order to avoid a noxious stimulus e.g. Isaacson and Wickelgren (1962) and Kimura (1958).

Theories concerning the role of the hippocampus in relation to behaviour have been surveyed in detail by Douglas (1967). One early hypothesis linked the hippocampus with emotional behaviour, largely on the basis of the marked emotional changes found in animals with the Kluver–Bucy syndrome after bilateral temporal lobe removals. Since the subjects in experiments using the more restricted medial temporal lesions, like those in the experiments already described, do not show the emotional changes associated with the Kluver–Bucy syndrome this hypothesis is therefore untenable. A second hypothesis which links the hippocampus to recent memory is particularly attractive in view of the evidence from human subjects like HM. Unfortunately, there is evidence from animal experiments which is inconsistent with the notion that hippocampal lesions cause deficits in recent memory. For example, Kimble and Pribram (1963) had their hippocampectomized subjects learn a visual discrimination and manipulated the intertrial interval. On the assumption that recent memory is impaired it would be expected that performance would deteriorate more with longer intertrial intervals but this was not found.

The most attractive theory, which is held by Douglas (1967) and Kimble (1969) is that the hippocampus is involved in inhibitory functions. This general theory has a number of possible variants which are discussed in detail by Douglas (1967). The difficulty that hippocampectomized animals have in passive avoidance-learning suggests that the subject is unable to inhibit an established response. Orbach *et al.* (1960) explain the ability of monkeys with medial temporal lesions to perform adequately in delayed response tasks but not on delayed alternation, as being due to the fact that in delayed alternation the subject is required to inhibit the previously correct response on every trial.

These experiments are ambiguous as to the exact nature of the postulated inhibitory process. It could be that the hippocampectomized subject is unable to inhibit an incorrect response or it could be that the hippocampectomized subject is unable to inhibit attention to cues that are irrelevant. Responding on the basis of irrelevant cues results in the incorrect response. Douglas and Pribram (1966) advocate this latter alternative and suggest that the hippocampus acts so as to diminish awareness of non-reinforced stimuli whilst the amygdala, another temporal lobe structure, acts to heighten awareness of reinforced stimuli. They also present a series of experiments relevant to their hypotheses.

Especially telling is a finding that monkeys with hippocampal lesions respond more readily to a stimulus previously associated with non-reward when this is subsequently paired with a novel stimulus. This suggests that the hippocampectomized subjects failed to register the significance of the cue that was not rewarded during the preliminary training. It would be predicted from their theory that hippocampectomized subjects would be slower to extinguish a learned response than normal animals and those with lesions in the amygdala. This was also demonstrated by Douglas and Pribram (1966).

Inferotemporal lesions

Lesions in the temporal neocortex, and in particular those in the inferotemporal region, also affect the learning of visual discriminations. These subjects are impaired on both simultaneous and successive visual discriminations with successive discriminations presenting the greatest difficulty (Pribram and Mishkin, 1958). In Pribram and Mishkin's experiment the successive discrimination problem required the subject to respond when one stimulus was presented, but to refrain from responding when the other was presented (a 'go-no-go' discrimination). Pasik *et al.* (1960) found no significant impairment post-operatively when the successive discrimination task did not require the subject to withhold from responding when one of the two stimuli was presented. As with hippocampal lesions, there is a suggestion here that the subjects may have difficulty in inhibiting responses. This notion receives further support from Schilder *et al.* (1968), who report that by far the largest proportion of errors on a 'go-no-go' discrimination task come from responses on the 'no-go' trials. Besides affecting visual discrimination-learning, inferotemporal lesions produce a deficit in the retention of discriminations acquired pre-operatively (Iverson and Weiskrantz, 1970) except when the discrimination is heavily over-learned in pre-operative training (Orbach and Fantz, 1958).

Although this deficit with visual discrimination tasks can exist independently of any visual field defect (Mishkin and Pribram, 1954) and inferotemporal lesions produce no loss of visual acuity (Weiskrantz and Cowey, 1963) there does appear to be some disturbance in the visual perceptual analysing mechanisms. Experiments by Butter (1968) and Iverson and Weiskrantz (1967) have shown that the inferotemporal monkey does not attend to the same attributes of the visual stimulus as the normal subject and Butter *et al.* (1965) have shown that the generalization gradient for both colour and spatial orientation of the visual stimulus is flatter in monkeys with inferotemporal lesions.

Butter *et al.* (1965) claim that the inferotemporal discrimination impairment is restricted to the visual modality but the relevant evidence is contradictory. Deficits in both auditory and tactile discriminations have been reported. Stepien *et al.* (1960) found both auditory and visual discrimination disturbances after bilateral excisions of temporal cortex and Schilder *et al.* (1968) found deficits in tactile discrimination. On the other hand, Cordeau and Mahut (1964) and Wilson (1957) respectively found no deficit on auditory or somesthetic discriminations. These inconsistencies cannot be resolved in terms of the types of discrimination task used (simultaneous or successive) but it is quite probable that the exact extent of the lesion will be critical in determining whether modalities other than the visual are involved.

With regard to drawing parallels with research on human subjects, experiments examining the retention of learned discriminations are of the greatest interest. Iverson and Weiskrantz (1964 and 1970) have shown that inferotemporal monkeys have difficulty in retaining learned discriminations over a period of twenty-four hours. In the more recent paper these authors found that even when the discrimination had been relearned there was still little retention over a further twenty-four hour period. Although there seems to be no evidence on this point, it is very likely that the degree of initial learning is an important variable in determining the amount of retention in these subjects. Iverson and Weiskrantz did not use a very stringent criterion for learning. They suggest that the findings mihgt be partly, but not completely, explained by the poor stimulus analysing and categorization in the inferotemporal subjects. This fact would lead to a difficulty in learning and result in an engram which would be less well defined and more susceptible to interference in storage. They also describe an unpublished study of Twai and Mishkin which purports to show that the visual pattern discrimination deficit is confined to the more posterior part of the region usually incised in inferotemporal lesions. The cited authors also have evidence suggesting that anterior areas involved in the usual inferotemporal lesion may be important for the normal functioning of memory. Thus the deficits found in monkeys with inferotemporal lesions may have both a perceptual and a memory component.

Summary and evaluation

In humans, a large number of different behavioural functions have been found to be impaired by temporal lesions. These include a lowering of measured intelligence, difficulties in the acquisition of new information and perceptual disturbances. Amongst the mass of information two features stand out:

1: The marked *difference* between the effects of right and left temporal lesions. The general pattern of the differences is to relate verbal functions to the left side and non-verbal functions to the right. Thus left temporal lesions are associated with a decline in verbal IQ, and difficulties in the perception and learning of verbal material. With right-sided lesions there is a decline in performance IQ and perceptual disturbances for material that is not readily coded in a verbal form. The functional asymmetry found in the temporal lobe reflects the general pattern of functional asymmetry found throughout the brain and this issue will be taken up again in the concluding chapter.

2. The very *severe memory disturbance* associated with bilateral medial temporal lesions in man. This very striking finding is not replicated in any comparable way by any of the varieties of temporal lobe lesion studied in animals. This discrepancy between animal and human studies has no obvious single cause. One important factor is that in the case of human subjects the very marked amnesia is for verbal material and, in the case of HM, some non-verbal tasks can be learned with a degree of facility even though this may not be up to normal levels. It would be interesting to examine the performance of both humans and monkeys with medial temporal lesions on comparable tasks.

The biggest source of difficulty in achieving a reconciliation lies in the mechanisms postulated to account for medial temporal deficits in men and animals. Those involved in studying cases like HM have not unreasonably implicated memory storage mechanisms. Short-term memory remains intact and the core of the problem seems to be the difficulty in getting material into long-term storage. On the other hand, animal researchers have been more attracted to theories involving inhibition. By making suitable additional assumptions it is possible to bring these two types of theory together (one such attempt is described by Douglas (1967) but this is not particularly convincing.

Recently Warrington and Weiskrantz (1970) have tried to reorient thinking about severe amnesic states in humans more along the lines of theorizing in animal research. The evidence presented by Warrington and Weiskrantz (1970) is difficult to evaluate in the present context because their experimental group of four subjects was not homogeneous with regard to diagnosis. One of these subjects had bilateral medial temporal lobe damage and is comparable to HM but the other three had alcoholic Korsakov states and presumably had lesions in different, though not unrelated, structures. We therefore have to accept Warrington and Weiskrantz's assumption, for which they have some good evidence, that the amnesic phenomena shown by these patients are all identical. In a series of ingenious experiments these authors show that despite very poor performance in the retention of learned verbal material when tested by conventional methods, the amnesics show normal retention when partial information is given at recall (e.g. initial letters of correct words). This led Warrington and Weiskrantz to suggest that amnesic subjects may get material into long-term storage adequately but that the information may not be correctly categorized or, that the amnesic subject is unable to inhibit incorrect information. If this analysis proves correct in the case of human bilateral hippocampal lesions then the interpretation of the effects of such lesions in both man and animals becomes very similar.

4 The Parietal and Occipital Lobes

Lesions of the posterior parts of the brain present a fascinating range of psychological dysfunctions. These are principally related to vision, the perception of spatial relationships and the somatosensory system. The different types of disorder that have been described in clinical observations are legion and anything approaching a comprehensive catalogue of them would more than exhaust the space available. A comprehensive coverage can be found in Critchley's (1953) extensive review of the parietal lobes and in the account of Gloning *et al.* (1968) concerning the disturbances they have found in a large series of cases with occipital lesions.

The present treatment of this area will therefore be a very selective one. It will be largely concerned with the more commonly encountered dysfunctions and those that have been subjected to more searching investigation than just clinical description. The general plan will be to begin with the examination of those disturbances of behaviour that are closely related to sensory functions and then to pass to the less well defined and more complex dysfunctions.

Visual field defects and their related perceptual disturbances

The visual pathways, which remain compact until they reach the lateral geniculate body, then radiate, sweeping out laterally until they finally reach the primary visual area in the striate cortex of the occipital lobe. Because of the anatomical distribution of the pathways, lesions in the posterior parts of the brain are liable to interfere with them and produce visual field defects.

Figure 3 indicates the general anatomical relationship between visual field defects and lesions in the posterior parts of the brain. It can readily be understood that, because of the hemidecussation of fibres in the optic pathways at the optic chiasm, unilateral lesions posterior to the optic chiasm produce field defects in the contralateral halves of the visual fields (hemianopias). Such defects may be complete or partial, depending on the nature of the lesion and are always homonymous. Visual field defects in the upper or lower quadrants only may be produced by the appropriately placed lesions as illustrated in Figure 3. It is also worth noting that in the case of homonymous hemianopias the macular, or central point of vision, is spared and reflects the fact that macular vision, unlike peripheral vision, is represented bilaterally in the cortical projection of the visual pathways. A detailed account of the relationship between different injuries to the brain and their consequent field defects is given by Teuber *et al.* (1960).

Of more direct psychological interest are the disturbances in visual perception which result from visual field defects. A large number of investigations into such perceptual disturbances have been described by Teuber and Bender (1949). They used as their subjects war casualties with penetrating missile wounds in the occipital region of the brain.

Two commonly occurring phenomena in their subjects were described as 'completion' and 'extinction'. (Teuber and Bender's use of the term 'extinction' bears no relationship to the usual meaning of the term in psychology.) If a simple pattern, e.g. a square, is projected into a patient's visual field such that part of the pattern passes over a scotoma, the subject may well report that he has 'seen' the complete square and not the shape minus that portion which corresponds to his defective area of vision. Such completion is enhanced by the rapid exposure of the stimulus.

The opposite of completion occurs in extinction. If a stimulus is projected to a part of the subject's visual field which is impaired but not totally blind, e.g. the left visual field of a patient with a right posterior lesion, he may report the presence of the stimulus in an apparently normal way. When this stimulus is paired with a similar stimulus presented simul-

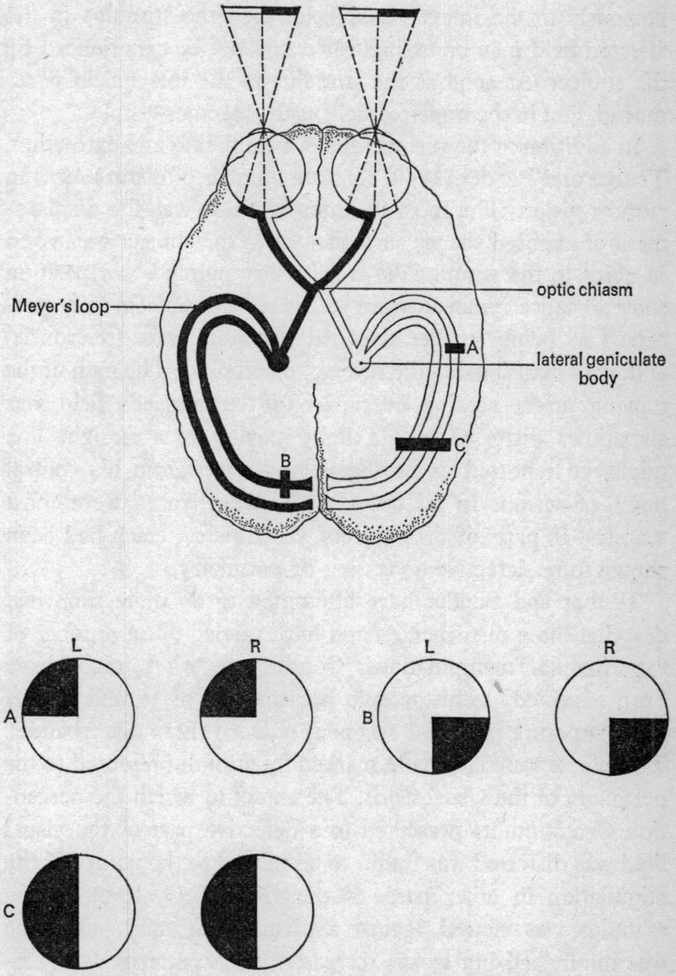

Figure 3 Diagram of the visual pathways showing the visual field defects produced by lesions at different places

taneously to the intact visual field, then the stimulus in the affected field may be extinguished and not be experienced by the subject. As soon as the stimulus in the intact field is removed, that in the impaired field again becomes visible.

In addition to the phenomena of completion and extinction, Teuber and Bender (1949) report a number of disturbances in pattern vision. The most common of these was the displacement of exposed shapes such that when the subject was asked to point to the stimulus he consistently pointed to a position some distance removed from it. Sometimes objects were perceived as being smaller than they actually were (micropsia) and, very occasionally, the reverse (macropsia). The path of the moving target passing over part of the subject's field was sometimes distorted, e.g. a light moving in a straight line might be reported as having curved away from his central point of vision. In all cases these disturbances were most manifest in parts of the subjects' visual fields which had been shown to be defective on testing by perimetry.

Teuber and Bender have attempted to do more than just describe these disturbances and have carried out a number of experimental manipulations. Contrary to what might have been expected, tachistoscopic presentation of stimuli with a short exposure time (0·1 seconds) reduced these disturbances. The effects were also more marked for stimuli presented to the periphery of the visual fields. The extent to which the perception of a stimulus presented to a defective part of the visual field was distorted was found to be related to the nature of the stimulation in other parts of the visual field. If the single stimulus was viewed against a plain background, distortion was minimized but it was increased when patterns were presented to the intact parts of the visual fields.

Others have subsequently investigated the phenomena of completion and extinction. Warrington (1962) presented geometric forms tachistoscopically to patients with homonymous hemianopias. Some of her stimuli consisted of the right or left halves of regular designs (circles, squares, crosses, etc.) which were presented such that the complete half of the design fell into the intact part of the subject's visual field. The missing half of the design, if it had been present, would have fallen into the hemianopic field. Just over half of her subjects exhibited completion and this occurred even for those stimuli consisting of only half a design presented into the intact field. This is a convincing demonstration that completion is a real phenomenon and not due to some power of vision being left in the affected field. Warrington found that completion was associated with lesions in either parietal lobe producing a hemianopia and of which, as is often the case, the subject is unaware.

With regard to extinction, Wyke and Ettlinger (1961) found that a patient with a right temporal lobe tumour, and consequent left upper homonymous field defect resulting from damage to the optic radiation as it passes through the temporal region, showed normal recognition of digits presented to each hemisphere separately in a tachistoscope. When digits were presented simultaneously to both right and left visual fields, the threshold for recognition was raised in the left field thus showing extinction.

A final phenomenon that has been related to visual field defects is rotation on the block design test (Koh's blocks). The basis of the test is a set of four or nine coloured cubes with different colour arrangements on each side. The subject fits these together to form a square design which matches the sample given by the experimenter. It has long been noted that brain-damaged subjects who may reproduce the design correctly, tend to rotate their copy of the design. Shapiro and his associates at the Institute of Psychiatry in London have reported an extensive series of experiments with this phenomenon and have related it to certain characteristics of the designs used. In their latest paper, Shapiro *et al.* (1962) show that this effect is dependent on the presence of visual field defects in the brain-damaged subjects.

Visual field defects are therefore related to a variety of disturbances in visual perception. One important implication of these disturbances is that they indicate that no one part of the visual field operates in isolation and that considerable interaction occurs between different parts.

Other sensory and perceptual disturbances

The parietal lobe includes at its anterior margin the post-central gyrus along which the various parts of the body are represented for purposes of sensation. In view of this, somatosensory disturbances may be expected to be prominent among the dysfunctions resulting from parietal lesions.

Phenomena comparable to those observed in the visual modality have been recorded. Bender (1952) has described both extinction and displacement in the somatosensory system. In the case of displacement, a tactile stimulus is usually reported as being more proximal than it really is. Following a unilateral lesion, a patient may be able to identify a tactile stimulus on the affected (contralateral) side of the body. When this stimulus is paired with one to the same place on the other side of the body, the first stimulus may fail to be reported.

Semmes *et al.* (1960), report the assessment of various sensory thresholds in patients with both unilateral and bilateral lesions due to missile wounds. Whilst unilateral lesions were found to produce the expected sensory changes for light pressure, point localization and two-point discrimination in the contralateral hand, it was found that left hemisphere lesions tended to produce ipsilateral changes also. The only exception to this was in the judgement of passive movement where the unilateral lesion, whether to the right or left hemisphere, was found to affect only the contralateral hand. A further interesting asymmetry in the effects of lesions to the two hemispheres was observed in that changes in these sensory thresholds were largely observed following lesions of the sensorimotor regions as far as the left hemisphere was concerned. In the case of the right hemisphere these changes were produced by lesions from all parts of the hemisphere.

A similar study to that of Semmes *et al.* (1960) is reported by Corkin *et al.* (1970) who investigated patients undergoing unilateral excision from various parts of the cortex for the relief of focal epilepsy. Corkin *et al.* conclude that lasting sensory loss occurs only with lesions of the post-central gyrus and that any sensory deficits resulting from lesions in other parts of the parietal lobe are only transient. They also found that a substantial minority of subjects showed sensory changes that were present in the ipsilateral as well as the contralateral hand. Unlike Semmes *et al.* they felt that ipsilateral changes were not related to the side of the lesion but tended to occur in those patients who had more extensive lesions.

Similar disturbances of somesthetic functioning must underlie the inability of many patients with brain lesions to maintain certain bodily postures in the absence of visual feedback. Wyke (1966) examined the ability of neurological patients to perform the commonly used clinical test of maintaining the arms stretched out horizontally in front of the body in absence of vision. The drift in the position of the arms over a period of thirty seconds was noted and it was found that such drift occurred in all patients with parietal lesions and in some with lesions to other parts of the brain. It was also found that right-sided lesions only produced postural drift in the contralateral arm whilst left-sided lesions also affected the ipsilateral arm although this was to a lesser degree than for the contralateral (right) arm.

Teuber and his associates (Weinstein, Ghent and Semmes) have carried out a number of other experiments related to somatosensory functioning. Although this is the most appropriate place to consider it, their research does not fit exactly into the present context because the groups of subjects used have lesions in various parts of the brain although posterior lesions are by far the most numerous. In some of the experiments where they try to examine the differential effects of lesions in difficult areas (e.g. Ghent *et al.*, 1955; and Weinstein 1955a) no differential effects are found. This is certainly partly due to the small numbers of subjects with different types of lesion but it is still true to say that the results described are not specific to lesions in the posterior parts of the brain even though this may be the region of maximum effect.

Weinstein *et al.* (1958) found that subjects with unilateral penetrating missile wounds were less able than controls to match samples of sandpaper by touch. They found that the left hand was more vulnerable to disturbance than the right, regardless of the side of the lesion. As might be expected, the subjects showing the most severe deficits were those with large lesions of the sensorimotor region, especially the inferolateral portion. These findings conflict with earlier investigations such as that of Evans (1935) who found that roughness discrimination was only impaired in the contralateral hand after unilateral lesions.

Judgements of the weight and size of objects placed in the hand have also been found to be impaired. Weinstein (1954) showed that changes in the judgement of weight resulting from unilateral injuries were dependent upon whether somatosensory changes were also produced. Where somatosensory changes were also present the weight was overestimated in the hand contralateral to the injury but underestimated in the contralateral hand when there were no somatosensory changes. Weinstein (1955b) further examined the judgement of weight in terms of negative time errors. Negative time error is a normal phenomenon in which the subject tends to judge the first two successively presented and identical stimuli, which are separated by a short time interval, as being less intense than the second. Weinstein noticed that subjects with parietal injury were particularly liable to show negative time errors in the judgement of weights. In the case of tactile size judgements, Weinstein (1955a) found that these were disturbed in the hand contralateral to brain injury but only in those patients who also had somatosensory impairment.

More complex tactile discrimination has been examined by Ghent *et al.* (1955) who required his subjects to learn to discriminate between shapes presented in the tactile modality. Their brain-damaged group, again all with unilateral lesions, were found to show comparable improvement to the controls in learning discriminations with the hand ipsilateral to the lesion but similar learning did not occur with the contralateral hand. In this instance the dysfunction was found to be related to other types of sensory disturbance.

Not unexpectedly, lesions in the parietal region have been shown to disturb performance on a number of tasks dependent upon the somatosensory system. In some instances, like a number of the somesthetic disturbances studied by Ghent *et al.* (1955) and the arm drift observed by Wyke (1966), lesions to the left hemisphere have been found to affect the left side of the body as well as the right. In contrast, right-sided lesions appear to be solely contralateral in their effects. Bender's (1952) demonstration of extinction for tactile stimuli indicates considerable interaction between the somatosensory systems subserving the two halves of the body.

Spatial abilities

Disturbances in the ability to appreciate spatial relationships are common following parietal lesions and a large number of different clinical manifestations have been described. These include such things as the patient's inability to distinguish right from left or to understand very simple maps and a number of bizarre but rare features like the complete neglect of one half of the external space. Experimental investigations of these phenomena are rather fragmented and do not cover the full range of clinically observed spatial disorders. For a detailed survey of the clinically observed described spatial disturbances the reader is again referred to Critchley (1953).

Semmes *et al.* (1955) conducted one of the earliest experiments. Their subjects were presented, either tactually or visually, with maps indicating a route to be followed by the subject in moving between a set of nine points marked out on the floor of the experimental room. Subjects with parietal lesions were found to be especially impaired on this task as compared with others who had lesions in other parts of the brain or with normal controls. The same authors (Weinstein *et al.*, 1956) later concluded that the disturbance in route finding was not attributable to a pure sensory deficit or to low general intelligence. Somesthetic deficits did tend to be more common amongst the subjects who performed worst on the test but Weinstein *et al.* (1956) argue that it is still necessary to conclude that the test reflects a definite deficit in route finding or spatial functioning in the group with parietal lesions, because these were equally impaired when the maps were presented visually as when they were presented tactually.

De Renzi *et al.* (1969) presented their subjects with an array of stimuli and tested their ability to remember the exact location of specific stimuli. Performance on this test of memory for position in space was impaired in all brain-damaged subjects for both visually and tactually presented stimuli. The subjects showing the greatest impairments were those with visual field defects and who were therefore likely to have posterior lesions.

Some investigators have attempted to assess the subject's ability to manipulate spatial relationships. One way of doing this is to present him with a visual stimulus and then to require him to indicate how this stimulus might appear when viewed from a different orientation or as seen in a mirror. Butters and Barton (1970) used several tasks of this type and found that performance was impaired in subjects with left or right parietal lesions but that little or no deficit was shown by subjects with lesions in other parts of the brain.

Another way of making the subject manipulate spatial relationships is to require him to transfer spatial information from one modality to another. One such experiment in cross-modal transfer was carried out by Butters and Brody (1968) who were concerned with testing out Geschwind's (1965a and b) hypothesis that the angular gyrus region (in the inferior parietal lobe) of the dominant hemisphere mediates cross-modal associations. Butters and Brody found that patients with left parietal damage were impaired in cross-modal association on tasks requiring visual-tactile, tactile-visual and auditory-visual matching. Only patients with left parietal lesions were used in this experiment but the evidence of Semmes *et al.* (1954) suggests that lesions in either parietal lobe can affect visual tactile matching and de Renzi and Scotti (1969) found that the maximum deficit in tactile–visual matching occurred in subjects with right posterior lesions. There is thus support for Geschwind's notion that cross-modal transfer, at least as far as spatial information is concerned, may be mediated through the left angular gyrus region but the structures of the right parietal lobe are also likely to be involved.

In discussing spatial orientation in patients with neurological disease a distinction has been drawn between orientation in external (extrapersonal) space and orientation with regard to the spatial organization of the patient's own body (personal space). Semmes *et al.* (1963) attempted to examine the relationship between these two types of orientation using the route finding maps of Semmes *et al.* (1955) to test extrapersonal spatial orientation. Personal orientation was assessed by requiring the subject to indicate on his own body certain points marked on diagrams of the human body. It was found that the two types of orientation were related and that performance on both tests were disturbed by left-sided posterior lesions. Subjects with left-sided anterior lesions were also impaired on the test of personal orientation but Teuber (1964) had advanced reasons to suggest that in the case of this group the poor performance can be better explained on grounds other than that of poor personal orientation. The task involving personal orientation required the subject to change set repeatedly between considering a diagram of the body that was facing him and one that was facing away from him. As we have seen in Chapter 2, subjects with frontal lesions experience difficulty in repeatedly changing set. There are therefore no empirical grounds for distinguishing between orientation in personal and extrapersonal space.

In conclusion, there is evidence of a wide range of disturbances in spatial orientation following parietal lobe lesions. In some of the cited experiments it might be possible to explain the findings in terms of more basic dysfunctions, e.g. sensory disturbances, but, taken together, the evidence is overwhelmingly suggestive of the parietal lobes being concerned with spatial orientation. De Renzi *et al.* (1971) suggest that this is due to the fact that most experiments have used complex spatial tasks like route finding. On using a very simple spatial test, that of judging the orientation of a single rod in space, de Renzi *et al.* (1971) found that patients with right posterior lesions were particularly impaired. It may well be that the important factor in determining whether an apparently spatial task is affected by left posterior lesions as well as right is the degree of verbal mediation used by the subject. Although a task may be spatial in nature, this does not prevent a subject from using verbal reasoning in its solution and to the extent that this occurs the task will be more liable to disruption by left-sided lesions, even though the task may be particularly difficult to verbalize.

Constructional apraxia

This term refers to an inability to put parts together to make a whole. Clinically, it is implied by a failure to perform adequately on such tasks as Koh's blocks (painted cubes which the subject is required to put together to form designs), the drawing of common objects and placing blocks of wood together to form three-dimensional objects. Recent reviews of constructional apraxia by Benton (1969) and Warrington (1969) give a history of the concept and an account of how it may be tested clinically.

The first question that must be asked about constructional apraxia is whether it is a single entity or just a descriptive term that can be applied to a large group of disorders of functioning which might reflect a number of different underlying disabilities. Benton (1967) attempted to answer this question by giving four tests alleged to reflect constructional apraxia (copying visual designs, stick construction, three-dimensional block construction and Koh's blocks) to a group of 100 patients with cerebral lesions. If constructional apraxia is a unitary dysfunction it would be expected that the four different tests would intercorrelate significantly. Unfortunately, the data derived from the tests did not permit a sophisticated correlational analysis but, on examining each test in relation to the other three, Benton was able to demonstrate a better than chance association between each pair of tests. Thus one of the necessary conditions for regarding constructional apraxia as a unitary characteristic has been met.

Assuming that constructional apraxia is a unitary dysfunction a number of other questions then become of interest. The ability to, say, construct a model out of wooden blocks involves a number of more basic processes like visual perception, manipulative ability, etc. It is therefore appropriate to ask if this disorder might be explained in terms of some such basic function. A second question concerns the extent to which constructional apraxia may be lateralized to one hemisphere or even pinned down to a particular anatomical region.

Some investigators (Piercy *et al.*, 1960; Piercy and Smyth, 1962) have claimed that when constructional apraxia is manifest in patients with unilateral lesions it is more common to those who have right-sided lesions. It is also claimed that when constructional apraxia occurs in cases with left-sided lesions it is also less severe than when it is associated with right-sided lesions. As Warrington (1969) points out, there are technical difficulties in these studies which make quantitative statements about the severity of disturbance very dubious and there is a very real possibility in most studies of unilateral cerebral lesions that the group with right-sided lesions will have a more extensive pathology than those with lesions on the left. The reason for this is that progressive lesions in the left may be more quickly noticed because they tend to affect speech. The factor of speech representation in the left hemisphere may also cause surgeons to be less radical in removing tissue when operating on the left hemisphere.

Arrigoni and de Renzi (1964) attempted to control these factors by equating the severity of lesions in their left- and right-sided cases. They used simple reaction time to equate for the severity of the lesions assuming, on the basis of experiments like that of Blackburn and Benton (1955) which show that reaction time is retarded in brain-damaged subjects, that simple reaction time is inversely related to the size of the lesion. After equating for severity of lesion in this way Arrigoni and de Renzi claim that the side of the lesion does not affect the incidence or severity of constructional apraxia. Unfortunately, this otherwise carefully executed experiment does not answer the question. The fact that reaction time can be reliably shown to be retarded after brain damage does not prove that there is a simple isomorphic relationship between reaction time and the size of the lesion. Even if such a relationship can be assumed, there is conflicting evidence about whether simple reaction time would be the best thing to use in this context (Miller, 1970).

Whether or not constructional apraxia is more common in cases with right-sided lesions, there have been some interesting attempts to show that the nature of constructional apraxia differs according to the side of the lesion that causes it. The evidence on this point is also relevant to the question of whether constructional apraxia owes its existence to a more basic dysfunction.

McFie and Zangwill (1960) examined eight cases with left-sided lesions in the posterior parietal region and a resultant constructional apraxia. They concluded that these left-sided cases tended to produce drawings which were a simplified version of the original that they were asked to copy but that they preserved the essential spatial relationships. This contrasts with previously reported cases with right-sided lesions where the drawings were fragmented and the essential spatial relationship is lost. Another study by Piercy *et al.* (1960) found that constructional apraxics with left-sided lesions were helped in their drawing of objects by having a model to copy from but right-sided cases were not. These two findings are probably pointing towards the same basic difference and further support comes from Arrigoni and de Renzi (1964) who found that it was only constructional apraxics with right-sided lesions who produced gross distortions of spatial relationships. Their left-sided cases, like those of McFie and Zangwill (1960) just simplified their drawings.

It is possible, for reasons given above, that the subjects with right-sided lesions in these investigations may have had a more severe dyspraxia and thus the observed differences may have been quantitative rather than qualitative. The simplification of drawings by the left-sided cases might be the first step towards the complete fragmentation of drawings seen in the right-sided cases. Warrington *et al.* (1966) ruled out this possibility by examining groups with right- and left-sided lesions matched for overall severity of constructional apraxia. Their assessment of the subjects was much more extensive than that of previous studies and a number of the differences predicted on the basis of these previous investigations were not upheld. However, some small differences between left- and right-sided cases were found, e.g. left-sided cases were more likely to make all the angles in the drawing of a cube right angles, and right-sided cases produced a greater asymmetry in their drawings. Nevertheless, the authors feel that the right-sided cases have a relatively greater difficulty in maintaining spatial relationships whilst the left-sided cases suffer from an inability to plan the drawing process which leads to oversimplification.

Although the conclusions about the qualitative differences in constructional apraxia resulting from left- and right-sided lesions have been reasonably consistent, the demonstrated differences have always been small. A more recent experiment, that of Dee (1970), was unable to demonstrate any differences at all. Dee concluded that most constructional apraxia is due to a disorder of visual perception irrespective of the side of the lesion but that there are a small proportion of cases where perception is normal and other explanations must be invoked. There is also no evidence that constructional apraxia can be explained on the basis of a decline in general intellectual functioning.

Constructional apraxia is a problem that has attracted a considerable amount of experimental investigation of the parietal lobes. Despite this the main questions relating to it have not yet been satisfactorily answered.

The Gerstmann syndrome

No discussion of parietal lobe symptomatology would seem complete without some mention of this alleged syndrome which was first described in its complete form by Gerstmann in 1927. The syndrome, consisting of a right–left disorientation, finger agnosia, acalculia and agraphia, is extensively reviewed by Critchley (1953) and is a much described and commented upon feature of posterior lesions.

It has rightly been pointed out by a number of commentators that if any group of signs is to be usefully designated as a special syndrome it is not sufficient to show that the signs can occur together in a number of individual cases. It must be demonstrated that, within the total complex of parietal lobe signs, this particular combination of four signs tends to cluster together such that if one of the four is found then this greatly increases the relative chance of finding the other three. If this criterion is not met there could be a meaningless proliferation of 'syndromes' referring to all possible chance combinations of signs and symptoms. On balance, Critchley (1953) comes down in favour of regarding the four components of the Gerstmann syndrome as not forming a configuration of special significance. This opinion is strongly supported by the experimental evidence of Benton (1961) who showed that the four components were not interrelated in the required way.

Whilst the term 'Gerstmann syndrome' continues to be used in the literature and may occasionally be useful as a descriptive term, it cannot be regarded as a cluster of signs of special theoretical interest.

Posterior lesions in animals

On the whole, investigators interested in the behavioural effects of brain lesions in animals have been rather less attracted towards the posterior parts of the brain than to the frontal and temporal regions. For this and other reasons, the amount of experimental evidence which relates directly to the sort of issues that have been examined in humans is quite small. The experiment of Eidelberg and Schwartz (1971) is almost unique in that it set out to elicit in monkeys a phenomenon originally described in man. They trained monkeys pre-operatively to discriminate between tactile stimuli to the right, left or both wrists and so were able to test 'extinction' as described by Teuber and Bender (1949). Lesions in a number of areas, including the post-central gyrus and posterior parietal cortex were found to produce extinction.

Lesions in the visual projection areas

Cowey and Weiskrantz (1963) have studied the visual defects resulting from striate cortex lesions in monkeys and have found results which are largely comparable to those found with humans. They point to a possible difference between monkey and man in that the monkey retains some sensitivity to flashes of light projected to 'blind' areas of the visual field. However, if may be that in man also the field defects produced by striate lesions are not absolute and Cowey and Weiskrantz cite some clinical observations in support of this.

The question of vision in monkeys with total striate cortex lesions has been investigated by Weiskrantz (1963) and Humphrey and Weiskrantz (1967) amongst others. Weiskrantz (1963) found that such subjects could discriminate visual stimuli on the basis of total luminous flux or total length of contour. Humphrey and Weiskrantz further showed that similar animals were able to detect and reach for objects especially when these were moving. These results indicate that, for the monkey at least, some analysis of visual information can be carried out at a more distal part of the visual pathway than the striate cortex and Humphrey and Weiskrantz suggest that it may occur at the super colliculus.

Visual and tactile discrimination

Wilson (1957) had monkeys with lesions in the parieto-occipital region attempt to discriminate the same shapes in both the visual and tactile modalities. Because these subjects were found to be impaired in the tactile but not the visual modality, Wilson argued that the deficit resulting from parieto-occipital lesions lies not in the appreciation of spatial relationships but is due to somesthetic disturbances. Similarly, Wilson *et al.* (1960) showed that monkeys with posterior parietal lesions were impaired in the learning of roughness discriminations and again concluded that the basic deficit was in somesthesis.

A similar sort of analysis was made by Ettlinger *et al.* (1960). They again found a deficit in tactile discrimination in monkeys with posterior parietal lesions and also noticed that their operated animals were impaired in the accuracy of reaching. Since there was a weak correlation between these two things, Ettlinger *et al.* implicate a motor dysfunction as the cause of poor tactile discrimination.

Whilst the evidence of these experiments is reasonably consistent, there are some conflicting findings. Bates and Ettlinger (1960) found impairments in both visual and tactile spatial discriminations in association with parietal lesions. If the finding of an impairment in the visual modality can be maintained in further experiments then a somesthetic or motor impairment cannot be the whole story of the basis of parietal dysfunction.

Ettlinger and Kalsbeck (1962) and Moffett and Ettlinger (1970) have been concerned with the effect of unilateral parietal lesions in the monkey. In both these experiments subjects were trained on tactile discriminations using one hand and then had lesions placed in the ipsilateral or contralateral posterior parietal cortex. Following retesting on the discrimination problems, some of the subjects were then given similar lesions on the hitherto unoperated side. The results of these two experiments were largely consistent in showing that impairment of tactile discrimination was produced by lesions which were contralateral and not ipsilateral to the hand being used. In the later experiment there was some evidence of an increased severity of impairment when the contralateral lesion was made bilateral but this finding was confounded by changes in hand preference in some of the subjects following the second operation.

Posterior parietal lesions in the monkey affect tactile discrimination and this seems to be related to sensory impairments in the somesthetic system. There is some evidence of an effect on visual shape discrimination but this is not confirmed by all investigators. Where the lesion is unilateral, the effect of posterior parietal lesions on tactile discriminations is confined to the hand contralateral to the lesion.

Concluding remarks

In man, lesions of the posterior parts of the brain have a fascinating variety of behavioural consequences. That visual and somatosensory disturbances occur is to be expected on anatomical grounds, but what could not be expected is the complexity of these dysfunctions, especially in the visual system. In so far as the relevant investigations have been carried out on animals, similar kinds of dysfunction have been found to occur but, as yet, no-one has satisfactorily demonstrated a disorder in the understanding of spatial relationships in the monkey comparable to that which is found in man.

As has been the case with the other major areas of the brain that we have considered, the parietal lobes exhibit some degree of asymmetry of functioning although there is some conflicting evidence with regard to this. Previously, the pattern of asymmetry has always been in terms of verbal versus non-verbal abilities and therefore it is of considerable interest that our survey of parietal dysfunctions has shown asymmetries that do not involve language. De Renzi *et al.* (1971) with their very simple task of positioning a rod found that lesions in the right posterior region of the brain were particularly sensitive in disrupting performance. Wyke's (1966) study of arm drift showed that a right hemisphere lesion only produced effects on the left side of the body but that left hemisphere lesions produced bilateral effects. A similar pattern of results was shown by Semmes *et al.* (1960) with somatosensory changes but the later investigation of Corkin *et al.* (1970) does not entirely confirm this asymmetry of somatosensory effects. Another important asymmetry lies in the fact that Semmes *et al.* (1960) found that somatosensory changes could be produced by lesions in most parts of the right hemisphere but only by lesions in a more restricted part of the left hemisphere. No convincing asymmetry has been demonstrated for more complex spatial functions like those involved in constructional apraxia.

Finally, it is worth repeating that the demonstration of such phenomena as extinction illustrates a considerable degree of interaction between the sensory analysing system of the two hemispheres.

5 The Split Brain

The two hemispheres of the brain must act together to control many forms of behaviour. Above the level of the midbrain, the necessary communication between the hemispheres can only occur through the forebrain commissures of which the corpus callosum is by far the largest and most important. Sectioning these interconnections between the hemispheres (the 'split brain') should provide information as to how the two hemispheres interact in normal functioning.

Producing a split brain in animals is a relatively straightforward procedure. The forebrain commissures and optic chiasm can all be sectioned to prevent any interhemispheric communication above the level of the midbrain. The split brain is much more difficult to study in humans although there is the rare congenital defect of agenesis of the corpus callosum. Unfortunately, in addition to their extreme rarity, cases of agenesis of the corpus callosum present the difficulty that the agenesis may only be partial and the condition is also often associated with other malformations of the brain (Loeser and Alvord, 1968). Some sections of the corpus callosum have been carried out on humans with severe epilepsy on the grounds that cutting the corpus callosum would prevent the spread of seizures from one side of the brain to the other and thus reduce the severity of attacks.

Many early observers of subjects with split brains were surprised to find that, despite all *a priori* arguments for the importance of the corpus callosum, its absence or sectioning failed to produce any drastic changes in behaviour. Sperry (1964) has remarked that these negative findings even caused suggestions, if only half seriously, that the only established function of the corpus callosum seemed to be to hold the two halves of the brain together or to transmit epileptic attacks from one side of the brain to the other. It is only since the pioneering work of Sperry and Myers in the 1950s that real progress has been made in analysing the functions of the corpus callosum.

Agenesis of the corpus callosum

This condition has been recognized for a considerable length of time but it is only relatively recently that reports of cases have contained anything of particular psychological interest. Russell and Reitan (1955) reviewed earlier reports of cases of agenesis of the corpus callosum and concluded that these suggested that the condition 'results in no mental impairment unless it is associated with other brain anomalies'. They hypothesize that this failure to show behavioural disturbances has been due to a failure of investigators to use properly standardized tests known to be sensitive to the effects of brain damage. They then report the detailed investigation of a nineteen-year-old girl with agenesis who showed a subnormal level of intelligence, a performance indicative of brain pathology on Halstead's (1947) battery, impaired visuomotor co-ordination and other behavioural abnormalities. Since we do not know what other anatomical malformations were present in this subject, and the indications from the case report are that there must have been others, it is impossible to relate the findings to absence of the corpus callosum alone. However, they do demonstrate that behavioural abnormalities, due to lack of the corpus callosum or other associated abnormalities, do occur in cases of agenesis of the corpus callosum.

Jeeves (1965) has carried out experiments with three cases of agenesis in which he claims that there is no evidence of other malformations of the brain. These subjects all had IQs that were below average and performed badly on visuomotor tasks. They were generally clumsy in movement and one subject showed no evidence of transfer of learning when a task involving only somesthetic cues was attempted with the hand not used for the original training. Jeeves also carried out two reaction time experiments. In the first the stimulus was a flash of light so arranged as to appear in one half of the visual field only and in the second the stimulus was a vibration transmitted through the surface on which one of the hands was resting. (It will be remembered from Figure 3 on p. 77 that information concerning visual stimuli presented to one half of the visual field will be transmitted to the contralateral hemisphere. Similarly sensory pathways from one half of the body cross over so as to relay information to the opposite side of the brain.) In both experiments 'crossed' and 'uncrossed' reaction times were measured, i.e. responses with the hand which was respectively ipsilateral or contralateral to the hemisphere which received the stimulus information directly. For both visual and tactile stimuli, the acallosal subjects were able to carry out 'crossed' reactions but these were relatively much slower than for 'uncrossed' reactions than was the case for normal subjects.

Another subject with agenesis of the corpus callosum has been studied by Bryden and Zurif (1970) who used the dichotic listening procedure with digits presented simultaneously to each ear. This subject showed a performance on the task which, in almost every detail, was indistinguishable from the normal controls. This result is surprising in view of the fact that previous experiments of this type carried out on subjects with sectioned corpus callosums had demonstrated differences between experimental and control subjects but these will be dealt with in a later section.

Apart from Jeeves (1965) who obtained convincing results in the expected direction, studies of agenesis of the corpus callosum have been disappointing. However, it must be re-emphasized that, since the agenesis is commonly only partial and usually accompanied by other malformations of the brain, unequivocal results would be difficult to obtain with this type of subject.

The split brain in man

Sectioning the corpus callosum for the relief of epilepsy was initiated by Van Wagenen and Herren (1940). Their cases were extensively studied by Akelaitas and his associates who reported their observations in a series of papers during the 1940s.

On the whole, this early work on split brain humans produced negative results. This was even the case when attempts were made to analyse the effects of presenting both verbal and non-verbal stimuli to the two halves of the visual fields (Akelaitas, 1941 and 1943). No major disturbances of gnosis, praxis or language were found (Akelaitas 1944). A number of reasons have been put forward to account for these unexpected results but, to the present writer, what is very noticeable about these papers is their apparent lack of sophistication in experimental technique. For example, it is not adequate just to present a stimulus to the left visual field and assume that the information will reach only the subject's right hemisphere, since the subject can move his eyes and bring the stimulus into other parts of his visual field. In order to perform this type of experiment satisfactorily it is necessary to expose the stimulus tachistoscopically in the required part of the subject's visual field with an exposure time that is less than the reaction time for eye movements (approximately 180 milliseconds). Akelaitas gives no indication that important points like this were ever taken into account in the design of his experiments.

A second group of investigators, principally Sperry, Gazzaniga and Bogen, have been experimenting with the series of commissurotomy patients operated on by Vogel in California. Their approach to the investigation of these cases has been similar in conception to that of Akelaitas but their techniques have been more sophisticated and the results much more interesting. A review of much of their work is to be found in Sperry (1968) and only a summary of the major findings will be given here. (Two useful primary references for this work are Gazzaniga *et al.* (1967), and Gazzaniga and Sperry (1967).)

These investigators found that a visual stimulus presented to one hemifield could only be recognized when presented to the same hemifield. Moreover the split brain subject can only verbally report what he has seen when the stimulus appears in the right visual field. Stimuli presented to the left visual field, and therefore transmitted through the right hemisphere, cannot be described verbally although the subject can indicate the corresponding object with his left hand. Similar phenomena are observed with stereognosis. Sensory information about an object placed in the right hand is dealt with by the left hemisphere and an unseen object placed in this hand can be named. The same object placed in the left hand cannot be described verbally but the left hand can retrieve an identical object by touch.

So far these results conform to the basic anatomical relationships and are consistent with the notion that, for the vast majority of persons, speech is localized in the left hemisphere. Sensory information reaching the left hemisphere can be described verbally. Such information reaching the right hemisphere can only produce responses of a non-verbal nature and, for both hemispheres, correct responses of a non-verbal nature can only be carried out by using the contralateral motor system. Under the experimental conditions used all transfer of information between the hemispheres appears to have been stopped by the split brain operation.

A number of other important questions emerge. One of these concerns general functioning. Everyday behaviour in acollosals is largely normal and, apart from such things as a minor degree of dyspraxia (Gazzaniga *et al.* 1967), deficits can only be observed under special testing conditions. IQ remains at the pre-operative level but short-term memory is depressed although some recovery occurs after about a year (Sperry, 1968).

Motor control is one very important issue since many of our everyday activities require the movement of the two halves of the body to be co-ordinated. Whilst the corticospinal (motor) tracts decussate at the level of the medulla there is a small group of fibres that do not cross over and therefore present the possible basis for some ipsilateral control of movement. The fact that major dyspraxic disturbances were not found in the Akelaitas series of investigations or by Gazzaniga *et al.* (1967) suggests that some ipsilateral control must occur. Sperry (1968) comments that ipsilateral control of limb movements is much better for proximal than for distal segments. He also reports an experiment whereby pictures of a hand in various positions are presented tachistoscopically to either visual hemifield and the subject is asked to mimic the picture with his own hands. The position in the picture is regularly copied by split brain subjects using the hand contralateral to the sensory input. With the ipsilateral hand performance is either very much poorer or breaks down completely.

A further point of interest lies in the functions that can be carried out in the right hemisphere. Gazzaniga and Sperry (1967) and Sperry (1968) describe a number of experiments which show that the minor hemisphere can carry out a number of symbolic tasks of a kind usually associated with the verbally dominant left hemisphere. In a situation in which the right hemisphere receives all significant sensory output and controls all responses the following were observed. There was a cross-modal transfer in that a stimulus presented in one modality could be matched with a corresponding stimulus in another modality. Logical association of generalization could occur in that if a visual stimulus, like a picture of a clock, is shown in the left visual field and the subject is asked to find a corresponding stimulus with the left hand then a related object, like a watch, will be identified if there is no clock amongst the objects that are left. Some capacity for very simple arithmetic can be shown, and the name of a common object presented to the left visual field can be matched with the corresponding object when felt by the left hand.

Some comprehension and manipulation of language and other symbolic material is therefore possible in the right hemisphere. Butler and Norrsell (1968) even report that a fifteen-year-old boy when tested after commissurotomy could occasionally name stimuli presented to the left visual field. This is the only recorded case of a split brain subject showing apparent initiation of speech by the right hemisphere. Other possible explanations of the results, e.g. that some of the stimuli might have been projected into the region of macular vision, were rejected by the authors. This finding of Butler and Norrsell is not so surprising when viewed against the background of Smith and Burklund's (1966) report of a forty-seven-year-old man who was occasionally able to produce coherent snatches of speech after a complete left hemispherectomy.

Although the performance of the right hemisphere is markedly inferior to that of the left on any task requiring the use of language, it is not the subordinate hemisphere for all functions. Following commissurotomy, even right-handed subjects are inferior at drawing objects in three dimensions, like the Necker cube or a house, and in carrying out the Koh's blocks test with the right hand as compared with the left (Gazzaniga *et al.*, 1965; Sperry, 1968). This reflects the superiority of the right hemisphere is handling spatial relationships.

Experiments involving the auditory modality have not yet been mentioned because of the complicating fact that it is not possible to limit the crucial auditory stimulus to one hemisphere in a manner that is analagous to those used for other sensory modalities. As we saw in Chapter 3 when discussing the results of dichotic listening experiments in subjects with temporal lobe lesions (pp. 60–61), information from each ear is transmitted to both hemispheres. Since the pathway from the ear to the contralateral hemisphere crosses over at the level of the brainstem it is not disrupted in the split brain subject.

Both Milner *et al.* (1970) and Sparks and Geschwind (1968) have carried out dichotic listening experiments with split brain subjects and agree that digits presented to the left ear are suppressed whilst those that are presented to the right ear are reported normally. Sparks and Geschwind explain their results by employing similar assumptions to those used by Kimura (1967) in her interpretation of the results of dichotic listening experiments after temporal lobectomy. Where conflicting information is presented to the two ears it is assumed that the contralateral pathway inhibits the ipsilateral one. Thus the left temporal lobe experiences the input from the right ear and the right temporal lobe that from the left ear. Where information arriving at the right temporal lobe is to be verbally repeated it is necessary for this information to be passed on to the left hemisphere over the corpus callosum. When the corpus callosum is sectioned this is not possible and so the information reaching the left ear is lost.

Sparks and Geschwind (1968) did find that with practice the degree of suppression of left ear stimuli decreased from 100 per cent suppression to 65 per cent suppression and suggest that the left temporal lobe can learn to discriminate and handle two separate inputs. This explanation also gives a possible basis for explaining the lack of suppression of left ear stimuli found by Bryden and Zurif (1970) in their case of agenesis of the corpus callosum although an alternative explanation, in terms of the agenesis being only partial, is always possible.

Much of the evidence considered so far indicates that the

two halves of the brain can function independently after section of the neocortical commissures. If this is the case, it should then be possible for the individual with a split brain to increase his information processing capacity by using both hemispheres simultaneously but independently. There have been two experiments relevant to this question. Gazzaniga and Sperry (1961) had subjects carrying out two simple discrimination tasks simultaneously. They had to respond with the right hand to indicate a red–green discrimination and with the left to indicate a light–dark discrimination. Reaction times for these discriminations were assessed both separately and simultaneously. Split brain subjects produced responses under the simultaneous condition as fast as for either of the discrimination tasks separately but normals decreased their reaction times by about 40 per cent under the simultaneous condition.

Gazzaniga (1968) reported an experiment similar in conception but using a short-term memory task. Letter sequences were presented to the right or left visual fields separately or simultaneously and subjects were tested for recognition of the letters that appeared. Split brain subjects appreciably increased the number of letters correctly recognized under simultaneous presentation as compared with presentation to either field separately. The increase for normal subjects was negligible. Given the appropriate experimental conditions, the information processing capacity of the split brain subject is increased but it is doubtful if this could ever be used to practical advantage since there is no possibility of co-ordinating the information in the two hemispheres.

Before leaving the work on the split brain in man, one point deserves to be made that has only been touched upon before. This discussion has emphasized the independent functioning of the hemispheres that can be demonstrated under appropriate and rigorous experimental conditions. The split brain subject appears to function normally under everyday conditions because sensory inputs are not carefully channelled into one hemisphere only. Furthermore, many investigators who have carefully studied split brain subjects report that these subjects develop some interhemispheric communication by means of 'cross-cueing'. An example will illustrate this. If the subject is required to name an object from a small group of familiar objects he has an obvious difficulty if the appropriate sensory input is restricted to the right hemisphere. The uninformed left hemisphere may then guess and give the name of an object in the group. If this guess is wrong the right hemisphere will recognize this and, say, initiate a shake of the head. This cue is picked up by the left hemisphere and another guess is made. Such cross-cueing may become quite sophisticated and difficult to detect.

The split brain in animals

Although the systematic investigation of split brain preparations has only occurred relatively recently there has been spasmodic interest in the effects of sectioning the corpus callosum extending back to experiments carried out in Pavlov's laboratory. Pavlov (1927) describes two experiments by Bykov using split brain dogs. In the first experiment, a dog with the corpus callosum sectioned was found to be unable to differentiate the side from which an auditory stimulus was presented, by learning to produce a conditioned response when a whistle was sounded on one side but not on the other. Normal dogs had previously been shown to be capable of acquiring this discrimination.

Bykov's other, more widely quoted experiment was based on the fact that when a conditioned response is established to a tactual stimulus applied to one place on the dog's body, this response will then generalize to similar tactile stimuli at other places including stimuli applied to the other side of the dog's body. Not surprisingly, Bykov found that sectioning the corpus callosum before attempting any training resulted in generalization of the conditioned response being confined to the same side of the body as that to which the conditioned stimulus was applied during training. This appears to have been the first example of a general finding that, with few exceptions, conditioning or learning mediated by one hemisphere fails to transfer to the other hemisphere in split brain subjects.

Subsequently a few experiments were carried out in other laboratories but there was probably no work of any importance on split brain animals between Bykov and that of Sperry and Myers. Myers (1955) in a preliminary experiment, used cats with only the optic chiasm sectioned. They were trained on a visual discrimination with one eye covered, thus restricting visual input to the hemisphere ipsilateral to the uncovered eye. Retesting, using only the untrained eye, showed good transfer of learning although the transfer was never complete. This demonstrates that some transfer of information relevant to the learned discrimination must occur between the two hemispheres. Both Myers (1956) and Sperry *et al.* (1956) carried out similar experiments using subjects in whom the corpus callosum as well as the optic chiasm had been sectioned. In these experiments no transfer of learning occurred between the trained and untrained eyes thus proving the importance of the callosal pathways for the interhemispheric transfer of learned discriminations.

Similar findings with regard to the significance of the corpus callosum have been obtained using other sense modalities and other species. Trevarthen (1962) carried out an ingeneous experiment on monkeys with both neocortical commissures and optic chiasm sectioned. His apparatus allowed each eye to view one of two conflicting sets of visual stimuli simultaneously. In this way the two hemispheres could be simultaneously trained to make two conflicting pattern discriminations. Under these conditions learning and retention were quite normal within each hemisphere, a finding which is impossible for the normal animal. Split brain cats and monkeys have been able to learn kinaesthetic discriminations with one paw as well as normal subjects but, unlike the normal subject, were unable to transfer this learning to the other paw (Ebner and Myers, 1962; Myers and Henson, 1960; Stamm and Sperry, 1957).

The two species most favoured for research in this area, the cat and monkey, have usually given results that are remarkably similar. However, one difference between the species that has emerged is that the role of the callosal system is much more highly developed in the monkey. We have already seen from Myers (1955) that interhemispheric communication in the cat is not completely efficient and the results of Myers and Sperry (1958) also suggest that in this species habits are more strongly entrenched in the directly trained hemisphere than in the hemisphere trained via the callosal projection. A much greater efficiency of learning transfer via the callosal system is implied by Glickstein and Sperry's (1960) experiment in intermanual transfer. Their normal rhesus monkeys were trained on a discrimination problem with one hand, then trained on its reversal with the other. On retraining with the first hand (and hemisphere), the reversed habit of the second hand (or hemisphere) was found to have shown good transfer and 'over-written' the original learning in the initially trained hemisphere.

Although the corpus callosum has been shown to be involved in the interhemispheric transfer of many different kinds of learning, it is not essential for all interhemispheric transfer. Meickle and Sechzer (1960) tested split brain cats on both pattern and brightness discriminations and found that, despite a completely sectioned corpus callosum, the brightness discrimination was transferred from one hemisphere to the other. No transfer of pattern discrimination was found. Trevarthen

(1965) has similarly found evidence of transfer of brightness discriminations in split brain monkeys which must occur via the midbrain. He suggests (Trevarthen, 1969) that the perception of brightness must be mediated by a different mechanism to that of pattern perception. This hypothesis is by no means proved by these results since it could be that inter hemispheric transfer of the simplest visual information can occur through the brainstem and that the brightness discrimination problems used in these experiments have been the simplest of all the tasks used. To test Trevarthen's hypothesis further and show that different pathways are responsible for different types of visual information, a double dissociation type of experiment would be required. If the technically difficult operation of sectioning the pathways in the brainstem responsible for the transfer of visual information could be achieved, then an animal with these pathways cut but with the neocortical commissures intact should be able to transfer a pattern but not a brightness discrimination. If this is so, different pathways must be involved for the two types of material, otherwise an explanation in terms of complexity of information is more plausible.

Critical parts of the corpus callosum

The corpus callosum is a very large structure and it is reasonable to expect that not all of its fibres will be involved in the interhemispheric transfer of any given types of information. To date, only one experiment (Myers, 1959a) has been directly concerned with the localization of function within the corpus callosum. In this experiment, Myers was concerned with the interhemispheric transfer of a visual discrimination in cats. Some of his subjects had lesions in the anterior parts and some in the posterior parts of the corpus callosum. Good transfer was found with anterior lesions but was absent in the case of large posterior lesions. There was some evidence of functional equivalence within the posterior parts of the corpus callosum in that small intact segments were able to support transfer irrespective of their position within the posterior corpus callosum. Although the report is not entirely clear from this point of view, Myers (1956) appears to have found that total sectioning of the corpus callosum or just the posterior two-thirds is equally effective in disrupting the transfer of visual discriminations in cats.

From anatomical considerations it is not surprising that it is the posterior parts of the corpus callosum that handle visual information. Comparable work relating to the callosal transfer of other types of information has yet to be done.

The nature of callosal transfer

The forebrain commissures can enable the interhemispheric transmission of information in two ways. Either the trained hemisphere can lay down engrams simultaneously in the trained hemisphere or the commissures can provide the means by which an untrained hemisphere can consult the storage system on the other side when it is presented with a problem. Myers and Sperry (1958) used chiasma-sectioned cats with one hemisphere trained on two visual discrimination problems, one of which was much easier to learn than the other. Following the completion of training, the visual cortex and surrounding areas were ablated on the trained side on the assumption that this would destroy memory traces on that side. On retesting using the untrained hemisphere, no transfer should occur unless the engrams had originally been laid down bilaterally since the memory store in the trained hemisphere is no longer there to be consulted. Myers and Sperry found good transfer of the easier, but not the harder problem, thus showing that, for the cat, the callosal pathways are only well enough developed for establishing independent traces in the other hemisphere during learning when the problem is simple.

Ebner and Myers (1962) trained four pairs of monkeys on a tactile discrimination with one hand. One subject in each pair then had the corpus callosum sectioned and training for all subjects was then commenced with the other hand. There were no significant differences between the subjects in the transfer of both easy and difficult tasks. It therefore follows, for this modality in the monkey, traces are established simultaneously in both hemispheres during learning.

Again further work on this problem is required. It is tempting to speculate on the basis of these two experiments that the higher species have a better developed callosal transfer mechanism whereby traces are always laid down bilaterally whilst lower down the phylogenetic scale, at the level of the cat, this is only possible for simpler information.

The corpus callosum and motor behaviour

The effect of transection of the corpus callosum and optic chiasm on the visual control of movement has been studied in a number of different experimental situations but the results have not been entirely consistent. Downer (1959) found that confining visual input to one hemisphere disrupted the visual control of movement by the ipsilateral hand. Conversely, Schrier and Sperry (1959) found that their cats with chiasma-commissure sections could reach out and press an appropriate stimulus object quite adequately with either paw despite the restriction of visual input to one eye. Myers *et al.* (1962) showed that cats and monkeys with the sensorimotor cortex of one hemisphere and the visual cortex of the other hemisphere ablated followed by sectioning of the corpus callosum were still able to perform tasks requiring eye–hand co-ordination of a crossed type.

Other experiments have trained chiasma-commissure-sectioned animals on visuomotor tasks using one particular eye–hand combination and then looked for transfer to other eye–hand combinations. Bossom and Hamilton (1963) trained their animals in reaching with the vision of the eye used in training distorted by placing a prism over it. The improved visuomotor co-ordination achieved after experience with the prism transferred to the other eye, but the hand used remained the same. Black and Myers (1965) and Kohn and Myers (1969) had monkeys with the same type of lesions learn to open latch boxes. Their results differed in that Black and Myers were able to show transfer from training with one eye–hand combination to other eye–hand combinations whilst Kohn and Myers (1969) could only show transfer where learning was binocular and transfer was from one hand to the other.

Most of these experiments agree in showing that visuomotor integration between the hemispheres can occur without the commissural system. Either information must be transmitted from hemisphere to hemisphere via the brainstem or, more likely, the necessary integration of motor behaviour must occur at the level of the brainstem.

Information processing in the split brain preparation

We have already seen that in split brain humans the amount of information that can be handled can be increased by getting the two hemispheres to process information independently. Gazzaniga and Young (1967) carried out a similar type of experiment using chiasma-commissure-sectioned monkeys. A display of four pairs of panels was presented independently to each eye. The subject's response was to press one of each pair of panels according to a light–dark discrimination after the total stimulus array had been lit for 0·2 seconds. The split brain subjects managed to learn to press all four correct panels on each side whilst the controls could only manage to get about two correct on each side. In one of the two split brain subjects the splenium had been left intact and this implies that it is the anterior portion of the corpus callosum that is responsible for inhibiting duplicate mechanisms in each hemisphere.

Concluding discussion

Sectioning the corpus callosum, and other forebrain commissures, produces a subject in which the two hemispheres can to a large degree function independently. This occurs to the extent that mutually contradictory information can be stored and acted upon by the two hemispheres simultaneously.

There are some exceptions to the general finding that the forebrain commissures are essential for the transmission of information between the two hemispheres and for the integration of the activity of the hemispheres. The animal evidence leads us to believe that the co-ordination of movement must take place largely in the brainstem. The study of split brain humans also indicates that some control of movement, especially in the proximal portions of the limbs, can be exerted through ipsilateral pathways. Animal experiments have also revealed that some visual information, in particular that relating to light–dark discriminations can be transferred between the hemispheres using extracallosal pathways.

There are two other features of note when the work on the split brain is considered as a whole.

1. As compared with the types of lesions discussed in previous chapters, there is a larger degree of consistency between the results of human and animal experiments. Thus we have a situation where there is a real possibility of using animal research as a way of understanding human functioning with the obvious exception of those functions that are dependent upon speech.

2. The split brain human presents a very powerful method for the studying of cerebral asymmetry of function. It is doubtful

if the evidence presented by Sperry (1968) concerning the capacity of the right hemisphere for understanding and using verbal material could have been so convincingly obtained from any other source.

6 A Return to Basic Issues

The preceding chapters have attempted to indicate the nature of the behavioural disturbances produced in man by localized brain lesions together with some consideration of related findings in the monkey and other experimental animals. The effects of lesions are so varied that a complete summary would become very tedious and any attempt to fit the evidence into any overall theoretical scheme is almost impossible. Rather than attempt this sort of analysis it seems more appropriate to examine a number of basic issues that have emerged, either explicitly or implicitly, in the previous discussions.

Asymmetry of function in the brain

Asymmetry of function is a major issue in neuropsychology. This is borne out by the fact that in all the areas of the brain that we have considered we have found evidence that the left hemisphere is not functionally equivalent to the right. To discuss this phenomenon using the traditional term 'cerebral dominance' implies a particular kind of functional relationship between the two halves of the brain whereby one hemisphere is subservient in all its functioning to the other, 'dominant' hemisphere. Piercy (1964) has argued that dominance is not the only possible functional relationship between the hemispheres and that evidence for other types of relationship does exist. Furthermore, the way in which the two hemispheres interrelate functionally varies according to the function being studied. (The concept of cerebral dominance grew largely out of a consideration of language and this still remains the function for which the term is most appropriate.) For these reasons the more neutral term of 'functional asymmetry' is to be preferred in discussing this general area.

The evidence surveyed points overwhelmingly towards a relationship between the left hemisphere and verbally mediated functions, whilst the right hemisphere is more related to visuospatial abilities. Various types of left-sided lesion have produced such deficits as a decline in verbal IQ, a loss of verbal fluency and an impairment in verbal learning and memory. The evidence from human split brain subjects confirms that the left hemisphere is involved in complex functioning and the control of speech. The evidence for right hemisphere specialization is not so striking but the accumulated evidence consistently shows the right hemisphere to be better adapted than the left for the perception of non-verbal material and the manipulation of spatial relationships. However, it must be remembered that hemispheric specialization for these functions is not complete, e.g. experiments with split brain humans have shown that some comprehension of speech can occur in the right hemisphere.

Two questions, neither of which can be fully dealt with here, arise out of the facts concerning asymmetry of functioning within the brain.

1. The relationship between hemispheric specialization for speech and hand preference.

2. The possible reason for this asymmetry of functioning.

In many of the investigations in which hemispheric asymmetry of function has been found the experimenters have been careful to use only right-handed subjects and the association between the left hemisphere and speech holds most definitely for dextrals. The picture is less clear for sinestrals and is also complicated by the fact that pure left-handedness is rare and mixed-handedness relatively common (Annett, 1967). According to Zangwill's (1960) survey of the problem, the proportion of subjects who are right-dominant for speech is very small and these are presumably found within the 4 per cent who in Annett's investigations turn out to be pure sinestrals. The general relationship between the left hemisphere and speech holds for the vast majority of subjects with the exception that, in mixed-handed subjects the capacity for speech in the right hemisphere is probably more developed than those who are purely right-handed. This latter proposition is borne out by Subirana's (1958) demonstration that non-right handers recover more quickly from aphasia than pure right-handers. It is also supported by Miller's (1971) finding of differential patterns of ability between normal right-handed and mixed-handed subjects.

The basic reason for asymmetry of function within the brain has not yet been worked out although there are a number of theories. The most interesting recent paper giving evidence of relevance to this problem is that of Semmes (1968) who reanalysed the data of the investigation of Semmes *et al.* (1960) into somatosensory changes following missile wounds. Semmes (1968) examined the findings in terms of the areas within each hemisphere that produced somatosensory changes. She found that such changes due to left-sided lesions resulted from lesions in the sensorimotor region whilst somatosensory changes due to right-sided lesions were related to lesions from all parts of the right hemisphere. On the basis of these findings she hypothesized that there is a focal representation of elementary functions in the left hemisphere and that this favours the execution of activities requiring fine sensorimotor control, like manual skills and speech. In the right hemisphere there is diffuse representation of elementary functions which favours activities requiring the integration of a large number of these elementary functions and hence the right hemisphere specialization for spatial abilities. Even if this theory is correct, there is still no complete explanation of asymmetry of function within the brain since we still have to explain the focal and diffuse representation of elementary functions in the two hemispheres. However, the theory does have the advantage that it brings the problem down to a more basic level than that of functional specialization for verbal as opposed to spatial abilities.

The relationship between human and animal studies

In discussing methodological issues in Chapter One the point was made that the limitations inherent in neuropsychological research with human subjects make the comparative approach of great potential interest. Unfortunately, we have seen that in practice, the correspondence between the behavioural disturbances produced by comparable lesions in humans and those in animals, especially primates, is not very great. The exception to this is the work on the split brain where the results obtained with the monkey and the cat are in substantial agreement with those obtained from split brain humans using non-verbal tasks. In the case of lesions in the major anatomical areas of the brain the results have often been quite discrepant but, nevertheless, it has sometimes been possible to point to ways in which thinking in human and animal research might coincide.

A detailed comparison of neuropsychological findings in man and the other primates has recently been made by Drewe *et al.* (1970). They rightly pointed to two major, but not unrelated, differences between human and animal research.

1. The experimental tasks used are quite different. Given the general feature of much psychological research that results tend to be specific to particular experimental situations, then a divergence in findings is to be expected on this count alone.

2. The human facility of language. This not only makes it impossible to have animal experiments analagous to those investigations specifically involving language in humans but it also complicates all experimental situations. This is because human subjects commonly use the mediation of language in the solutions of problems that are overtly non-verbal in nature, e.g. a series of designs may not be remembered by their spatial characteristics but by their verbal descriptions.

It is therefore true to say that, if we are primarily interested in human neuropsychology, the comparative method has not been of great value and is likely to be of only limited value in the future. However, it is possible to be over pessimistic on this issue, and, given research on both humans and animals which attempts to use experimental techniques that are as similar as possible, research on the infra-human primates may yet make a useful contribution towards the understanding of human behavioural abnormalities.

Anatomical considerations

In the first few pages of this volume we came across the very fundamental question of the extent to which the so-called 'higher cortical functions' can be localized within the brain. The evidence we have considered subsequently has further supported the opinion presented earlier: that there is some degree of localization of function in that the effects of lesions do vary considerably according to the locus of the lesion. It has not supported the notion that it is sensible to conceive that there is a simple one-to-one relationship between parts of the brain and specific functions.

Geschwind (1965a; 1965b) has made an original and stimulating attempt to account for a large range of behavioural phenomena within an anatomical framework by means of the 'disconnection syndromes'. He starts from 'Flechsig's rule' that primary sensory regions of the cortex only have cortical connections with the adjacent association areas. These adjacent association areas are extensively connected to other parts of the cortex, both within the same hemisphere and with the cortex of the other hemisphere via the callosal system. These intercortical connections provide the essential links between the various afferent and efferent systems and the limbic system.

Geschwind argues that, because of these anatomical features, lesions of the association areas can be considered as having the effect of disconnecting one or more sensory or efferent systems from the rest. This then provides a basis for understanding many neuropsychological disturbances. Thus Geschwind concludes on the basis of both anatomical and behavioural evidence that the agnosias are 'modality specific naming-defects' in which the appropriate sensory cortex has had its links with the speech areas broken.

The approach of the disconnection syndromes provides a potentially powerful way of analysing the effects of localized brain lesions. To date, Geschwind and his associates have applied it largely to the more unusual syndromes within the agnosias, apraxias and aphasias and its effectiveness in more widespread applications remains to be seen.

The influence of sub-cortical structures

The work cited in this volume has been largely concerned with the effects of lesions within the major cortical areas of the brain. As was explained in the opening chapter, this reflects the pattern of published investigations in this field. It is, of course, true that very few lesions are confined solely to the cortex and in discussing the effects of lesions in any particular cortical area we have been concerned with the effects of damage to the cortex and its underlying white matter.

Nevertheless, it is the case that sub-cortical structures, like the hypothalamus and the arousal systems originating in the brainstem, which are extremely important in the control of behaviour, have been neglected. By far the greatest proportion of work on the sub-cortical mechanisms underlying behaviour has been carried out in the animal laboratories of the physiological psychologists and has therefore come outside the scope of this book with its emphasis on the lesions found in human subjects. Accounts of research on sub-cortical structures can be found in the standard textbooks of physiological psychology and a useful introduction specifically concerned with this area is given by McCleary and Moore (1965).

A recent development in the study of sub-cortical lesions that does relate closely to the other investigations described in this volume is the study of thalamic lesions in humans. Patients with Parkinson's disease (a condition associated with an involuntary tremor in the limbs but which can also produce other motor disturbances) are sometimes treated surgically, usually by the placing of small lesions within the ventrolateral nucleus of the thalamus. Besides producing beneficial changes in the motor symptoms of this condition, the lesions have also been found to produce minor changes in cognitive and other functions. The findings are too complex to summarize meaningfully in a few sentences but the most prolific writers in this area, Riklan and his associates in New York, have provided an extensive review of their work (Riklan and Levita, 1969).

Future pospects

Neuropsychological investigation has increased tremendously over the past two decades. An indication of the expansion of knowledge within this field during the period of a little over a decade prior to the writing of this volume, can be obtained by comparing the contents of this volume with that of the review of the effects of brain damage given by Meyer (1960).

Further knowledge will no doubt continue to accrue but two possible areas of development seem to the writer to be now of potential importance.

1. Application of this knowledge to clinical problems. Psychologists interested in the effects of brain lesions have been largely motivated by theoretical considerations. There has been some attempt to use the knowledge obtained in the diagonsis of brain pathology but, since the radiological and other diagnostic techniques available to the modern neurologist are

much more effective, there is not much practical value in the psychologist being heavily committed to the diagnostic exercise except for a very limited range of conditions. A much more appropriate approach would be to try to apply knowledge of neuropsychological disturbances to the rehabilitation of brain-damaged patients such as those who have suffered strokes or severe head injuries. So far there has been little interest in rehabilitation but a notable exception is the Russian neuropsychologist, A. R. Luria. An account of Luria's work and ideas on rehabilitation can be found in Luria *et al.* (1969).

2. Relationship to general experimental psychology. Since subjects with brain lesions often develop disturbances in functions like memory, learning and perception which have been of especial interest to experimental psychology, they provide interesting, and potentially important evidence with respect to the experimental psychologist's theories of normal functioning. If a theory of normal functioning is correct then it is reasonable to expect that breakdown in this function following brain injury should bear some relation to the mechanisms proposed by the theory. A good example here is memory where it is generally considered that this is a two-stage process with information first entering a temporary, short-term store before being passed into a long-term store. The evidence we have considered relating to amnesic disturbances in patients with various types of temporal lobe lesions is consistent with this view. On the other hand, it is significant that Shallice and Warrington (1970) have described a detailed investigation of a case with a left parietal lesion in whom they claim there is an intact long-term store but a severely impaired short-term store. If the analysis is correct this case contradicts the usual assumption that the two memory stores must act in series and implies that input to the short-term and long-term stores must occur in parallel.

The nature of new ideas or insights in any science is notoriously difficult to predict. Irrespective of whether or not the two areas of development suggested above do prove to be of increasing importance, it is certain that the study of the psychological consequences of brain damage will continue to be fruitful. This work will play its part alongside the attainments of the many other disciplines involved in brain research in eventually reaching a comprehensive understanding of nature's highest achievement, the human brain.

References

AKELAITAS, A. J. (1941), 'Studies on the corpus callosum. II. The higher visual functions in each homonymous field following complete section of the corpus callosum', *Arch. Neurol. Psychiat.*, vol. 45, p. 788.

AKELAITAS, A. J. (1943), 'Studies on the corpus callosum. VII. Study of language functions (tactile and visual lexia and graphia) unilaterally following section of the corpus callosum', *J. Neuropath. exper. Neurol.*, vol. 2, p. 226.

AKELAITAS, A. J. (1944), 'A study of gnosis, praxis and language following section of the corpus callosum and anterior commissure', *J. Neurosurg.*, vol. 1, p. 94.

ALLISON, H. W., and ALLISON, S. G. (1954), 'Personality changes following transorbital lobotomy', *J. abnorm. soc. Psychol*, vol. 49, p. 219.

ANNETT, M. (1967), 'The binomial distribution of right, mixed and left handedness', *Quart. J. exp. Psychol.*, vol. 19, p. 327.

ARRIGONI, G., and DE RENZI, E. (1964), 'Constructional apraxia and hemispheric locus of lesion', *Cortex*, vol. 1, p. 170.

BATES, J. A. V., and ETTLINGER, G. (1960), 'Posterior biparietal ablations in the monkey', *Arch. Neurol.*, vol. 3, p. 177.

BENDER, M. B. (1952), *Disorders in Perception*, C. C. Thomas.

BENTON, A. L. (1961), 'The fiction of the "Gerstmann Syndrome" ', *J. Neurol. Neurosurg. Psychiat.*, vol. 24, p. 176.

BENTON, A. L. (1967), 'Constructional apraxia and the minor hemisphere', *Conf. Neurol. (Basel)*, vol. 29, p. 1.

BENTON, A. L. (1968), 'Differential behavioural effects of frontal lobe disease', *Neuropsychol.*, vol. 6, p. 53.

BENTON, A. L. (1969), 'Constructional apraxia; some unanswered questions', in A. L. Benton (ed.), *Contributions to Clinical Neuropsychology*, Aldine.

BLACK, P., and MYERS, R. E. (1965), 'A neurological investigation of eye-hand control in the chimpanzee', in G. Ettlinger (ed.), *Functions of the Corpus Callosum*, Churchill.

BLACKBURN, H. L., and BENTON, A. L. (1955), 'Simple and choice reaction time in cerebral disease', *Conf. Neurol. (Basel)*, vol. 15, p. 327.

BLAKEMORE, C. B., and FALCONER, M. (1967), 'Long-term effects of anterior temporal lobectomy on certain cognitive functions', *J. Neurol. Neurosurg. Psychiat.*, vol. 30, p. 364.

BLUMER, D., and WALKER, A. E. (1967), 'Sexual behaviour in temporal lobe epilepsy', *Arch. Neurol.*, vol. 16, p. 37.

BOSSOM, J., and HAMILTON, C. R. (1963), 'Interocular transfer of prism-altered co-ordination in split-brain monkeys', *J. comp. physiol. Psychol.*, vol. 56, p. 769.

BROADBENT, D. E. (1954), 'The role of auditory localization and attention in memory span', *J. exp. Psychol.*, vol. 47, p. 191.

BRYDEN, M. P., and ZURIF, E. B. (1970), 'Dichotic listening performance in a case of agenesis of the corpus callosum', *Neuropsychol.*, vol. 8, p. 371.

BUTLER, S. R., and NORRSELL, U. (1968), 'Vocalization possibly initiated by the minor hemisphere', *Nature*, vol. 220, p. 793.

BUTTER, C. M. (1968), 'The effect of discrimination-training on pattern equivalence in monkeys with inferotemporal and lateral striate lesions', *Neuropsychol.*, vol. 6, p. 27.

BUTTER, C. M., MISHKIN, M., and ROSVOLD, H. E. (1965), 'Stimulus generalization in monkeys with inferotemporal lesions and lateral occipital lesions', in D. I. Mostofsky (ed.), *Stimulus Generalization*, Stanford University Press.

BUTTERS, N., and BARTON, M. (1970), 'Effect of parietal lobe damage on the performance of reversible operations in space', *Neuropsychol.*, vol. 8, p. 205.

BUTTERS, N., and BRODY, B. A. (1968), 'The role of the left parietal lobe in the mediation of intra- and cross-modal associations', *Cortex*, vol. 4, p. 328.

BUTTERS, N., SAMUELS, I., GOODGLASS, H., and BRODY, B. (1970), 'Short-term visual and auditory memory disorders after parietal and frontal lobe damage', *Cortex*, vol. 6, p. 440.

CORDEAU, J. P., and MAHUT, H. (1964), 'Some long-term effects of temporal lobe resections on auditory and visual discrimination in monkeys', *Brain*, vol. 87, p. 117.

CORKIN, S. (1965), 'Tactually guided maze-learning in man: effects of unilateral cortical excisions and bilateral hippocampal lesions', *Neuropsychol.*, vol. 3, p. 339.

CORKIN, S. (1968), 'Acquisition of motor skill after bilateral medial temporal lobe excision', *Neuropsychol.*, vol. 6, p. 255.

CORKIN, S., MILNER, B., and RASMUSSEN, T. (1970), 'Somatosensory thresholds: contrasting effects of postcentral-gyrus and posterior parietal-lobe excisions', *Arch. Neurol.*, vol. 23, p. 41.

CORRELL, R. E., and SCOVILLE, W. B. (1965) 'Effects of medial temporal lesions on visual discrimination performance', *J. comp. physiol. Psychol.*, vol. 60, p. 175.

COWEY, A., and WEISKRANTZ, L. (1963), 'A perimetric study of visual field defects in monkeys', *Quart. J. exp. Psychol.*, vol. 15, p. 91.

CRITCHLEY, M. (1953), *The Parietal Lobes*, Arnold.

CROWN, S. (1952), 'An experimental study of psychological changes following prefrontal lobotomy', *J. Gen. Psychol.*, vol. 47, p. 3.

CROWN, S. (1953), 'Psychological changes following operations on the human frontal lobe'. *J. Consult. Psychol.*, vol. 17, p. 92.

DEE, H. L. (1970), 'Visuoconstructive and visuoperceptive deficit in patients with unilateral cerebral lesions', *Neuropsychol.*, vol. 8, p. 305.

DEETS, A. C., HARLOW, H. F., SINGH, S. D., and BLOMQUIST, A. J. (1970), 'Effects of bilateral lesions of the frontal granular cortex on the social behavior of rhesus monkeys', *J. comp. physiol. Psychol.*, vol. 72, p. 452.

DE RENZI, E., FAGLIONI, P., and SCOTTI, G. (1969), 'Impairment of memory for position following brain damage', *Cortex*, vol. 5, p. 274.

DE RENZI, E., FAGLIONI, P., and SCOTTI, G. (1971), 'Judgement of spatial orientation in patients with focal brain damage', *J. Neurol. Neurosurg. Psychiat.*, vol. 34, p. 489.

DE RENZI, E., and SCOTTI, G. (1969), 'The influence of spatial disorders in impairing tactual discrimination of shapes', *Cortex*, vol. 5, p. 53.

DORFF, J. E., MIRSKY, A. F., and MISHKIN, M. (1965), 'Effects of unilateral temporal lobe removals in man on tachistoscopic recognition in the left and right visual fields', *Neuropsychol.*, vol. 3, p. 39.

DOUGLAS, R. J. (1967), 'The hippocampus and behavior', *Psychol. Bull.*, vol. 67, p. 416.

DOUGLAS, R. J., and PRIBRAM, K. H. (1966), 'Learning and limbic lesions', *Neuropsychol.*, vol. 4, p. 197.

DOWNER, J. L. de C. (1959), 'Changes in visually guided behaviour following midsagittal division of the optic chiasm and corpus callosum in monkey (macaca mulatta)', *Brain*, vol. 82, p. 251.

DRACHMAN, D. A., and ARBIT, J. (1966), 'Memory and the hippocampal complex', *Arch. Neurol.*, vol. 15, p. 52.

DREWE, E. A., ETTLINGER, G., MILNER, A. D., and PASSINGHAM, R. E. (1970), 'A comparative review of the results of neuropsychological research on man and monkey', *Cortex*, vol. 6, p. 129.

EBNER, F. F., and MYERS, R. E. (1962), 'Corpus callosum and the interhemispheric transmission of tactual learning', *J. Neurophysiol.*, vol. 25, p. 380.

EIDELBERG, E., and SCHWARTZ, A. S. (1971), 'Experimental analysis of extinction phenomenon in monkeys', *Brain*, vol. 94, p. 91.

ETTLINGER, G., and KALSBECK, J. E. (1962), 'Changes in tactile discrimination and in visual reaching after successive and simultaneous bilateral posterior parietal lesions in the monkey', *J. Neurol. Neurosurg. Psychiat.*, vol. 25, p. 256.

ETTLINGER, G., MORTON, H. B., and MOFFETT, A. (1960), 'Tactile discrimination performance in the monkey: the effect of bilateral posterior parietal and lateral frontal ablations, all of callosal section', *Cortex*, vol. 2, p. 5.

EVANS, J. P. (1935), 'A study of the sensory defects resulting from excision of the cerebral substance in humans', *Proc. Ass. Nerv. Ment. Dis.*, vol. 15, p. 331.

FALCONER, M. A., HILL, D., MEYER, V., MITCHELL, W., and POND, D. A. (1955), 'Treatment of temporal lobe epilepsy by temporal lobectomy' *Lancet*, vol. 1, p. 827.

FALCONER, M. A., and WILSON, J. L. (1958), 'Visual changes following anterior temporal lobectomy: their significance in relation to "Meyer's loop" of the optic radiation', *Brain*, vol. 81, p. 1.

FINAN, J. L. (1942), 'Delayed response with pre-delay reinforcement in monkeys after the removal of the frontal lobes', *Amer. J. Psychol.*, vol. 55, p. 202.

FREEMAN, W., and WATTS, J. (1942), *Psychosurgery*, C. C. Thomas.

GAZZANIGA, M. S. (1968), 'Short-term memory and brain-bisected man', *Psychonomic Sci.*, vol. 12, p. 161.

GAZZANIGA, M. S., BOGEN, J. E., and SPERRY, R. W. (1965), 'Observations on visual perception after disconnexion of the cerebral hemispheres in man', *Brain*, vol. 88, p. 221.

GAZZANIGA, M. S., BOGEN, J. E., and SPERRY, R. W. (1967), 'Dyspraxia following division of the cerebral commissures', *Arch. Neurol.*, vol. 16, p. 606.

GAZZANIGA, M. S., and SPERRY, R. W. (1961), 'Simultaneous double discrimination response following brain bisection', *Psychonomic Sci.*, vol. 4, p. 262.

GAZZANIGA, M. S., and SPERRY, R. W. (1967), 'Language after section of the cerebral commissures', *Brain*, vol. 90, p. 131.

GAZZANIGA, M. S., and YOUNG, E. D. (1967), 'Effects of commissurotomy on the processing of increasing visual information', *Exper. Brain. Res.*, vol. 3, p. 368.

GERBOTH, R. (1950), 'A study of the two forms of the Wechsler-Bellevue Intelligence Scale', *J. Consult. Psychol.*, vol. 14, p. 365.

GESCHWIND, N. (1965a), 'Disconnexion syndromes in animals and man: Part I', *Brain*, vol. 88, p. 237.

GESCHWIND, N. (1965b), 'Disconnexion syndromes in animals and man: Part II', *Brain*, vol. 88, p. 585.

GHENT, L., MISHKIN, M., and TEUBER, H.-L. (1962), 'Short-term memory after frontal lobe injury in man', *J. comp. physiol. Psychol.*, vol. 55, p. 705.

GHENT, L., WEINSTEIN, S., SEMMES, J., and TEUBER, H.-L. (1955), 'Effects of unilateral brain injury in man on learning of a tactual discrimination', *J. comp. physiol. Psychol.*, vol. 48, p. 478.

GLICKSTEIN, M., and SPERRY, R. W. (1960), 'Intermanual somesthetic transfer in split-brain rhesus monkeys', *J. comp. physiol. Psychol.*, vol. 53, p. 322.

GLONING, I., GLONING, K., and HOFF, H. (1968), *Neuropsychological Symptoms and Syndromes in Lesions of the Occipital Lobe and Adjacent Areas*, Gauthier-Villars.

GOL, A., and FAIBISH, G. M. (1967), 'Effects of human hippocampal ablation', *J. Neurosurg.*, vol. 26, p. 390.

GOLDMAN, P. S., LODGE, A., HAMMER, L. R., SEMMES, J., and MISHKIN, M. (1968), 'Critical flicker frequency after unilateral temporal lobectomy in man' *Neuropsychol.*, vol. 6, p. 355.

GOLLIN, E. S. (1960), 'Developmental studies of visual recognition of incomplete objects', *Percept. Motor Skills*, vol. II, p. 289.

GREGORY, R. L. (1961), 'The brain as an engineering problem', in W. H. Thorpe and O. L. Zangwill (eds.), *Current Problems in Animal Behaviour*, Cambridge University Press.

GRIFFITH, H., and DAVIDSON, M. (1966), 'Long-term changes in intellect and behaviour after hemispherectomy', *J. Neurol. Neurosurg. Psychiat.*, vol. 29, p. 571.

GROSS, C. G. (1963), 'Locomotor activity under various stimulus conditions following partial lateral frontal cortical lesions in monkeys', *J. comp. physiol. Psychol.*, vol. 56, p. 232.

GROSS, C. G., and WEISKRANTZ, L. (1962), 'Evidence for dissociation of impairment in auditory discrimination and delayed response following lateral frontal lesions in monkeys', *Exper. Neurol.*, vol. 5, p. 453.

GROSSMAN, S. P. (1967), *A Textbook of Physiological Psychology*, Wiley.

HALSTEAD, W. C. (1947), *Brain and Intelligence*, University of Chicago Press.

HAMLIN, R. M. (1970), 'Intellectual function fourteen years after frontal lobe surgery', *Cortex*, vol. 6, p. 299.

HEBB, D. O. (1945), 'Man's frontal lobes', *Arch. Neurol. Psychiat.*, vol. 54, p. 10.

HIERONS, R., and SAUNDERS, M. (1966), 'Impotence in patients with temporal lobe lesions', *Lancet*, vol. 2, p. 761.

HUMPHREY, N. K., and WEISKRANTZ, L. (1967), 'Vision in monkeys after removal of the striate cortex', *Nature*, vol. 215, p. 595.

HUNTER, W. S. (1930), 'A consideration of Lashley's theory of equipotentiality of cerebral action', *J. Gen. Psychol.*, vol. 3, p. 455.

ISAACSON, R. L., and WICKLEGREN, W. D. (1962), 'Hippocampal ablation and passive avoidance', *Science*, vol. 138, p. 1104.

IVERSON, S. D., and WEISKRANTZ, L. (1964), 'Temporal lobe lesions and memory in the monkey', *Nature*, vol. 201, p. 740.

IVERSON, S. D., and WEISKRANTZ, L. (1967), 'Perception of redundant cues by monkeys with inferotemporal lesions', *Nature*, vol. 214, p. 241.

IVERSON, S. D., and WEISKRANTZ, L. (1970), 'An investigation of a possible memory defect produced by inferotemporal lesions in the baboon', *Neuropsychol.*, vol. 8, p. 21.

JACOBSEN, C. F. (1936), 'The functions of the frontal association areas in monkeys', *Comp. Psychol. Monogr.*, vol. 13, p. 3.

JEEVES, M. A. (1965), 'Psychological studies of three cases of congenital agenesis of the corpus callosum', in G. Ettlinger (ed.), *Functions of the Corpus Callosum*, Churchill.

KIMBLE, D. P. (1963), 'The effects of bilateral hippocampal lesions in rats', *J. comp. physiol. Psychol.*, vol. 56, p. 273.

KIMBLE, D. P. (1969), 'Possible inhibitory functions of the hippocampus', *Neuropsychol.*, vol. 7, p. 235.

KIMBLE, D. P., and PRIBRAM, K. H. (1963), 'Hippocampectomy and behavior sequences', *Science*, vol. 139, p. 824.

KIMURA, D. (1958), 'Effects of selective hippocampal damage on avoidance behavior in the rat', *Canad. J. Psychol.*, vol. 12, p. 213.

KIMURA, D. (1961a), 'Some effects of temporal lobe damage on auditory perception', *Canad. J. Psychol.*, vol. 15, p. 156.

KIMURA, D. (1961b), 'Cerebral dominance and the perception of verbal stimuli,' *Canad. J. Psychol.*, vol. 15, p. 166.

KIMURA, D. (1963), 'Right temporal lobe damage', *Arch Neurol.*, vol. 8, p. 264.

KIMURA, D. (1967), 'Functional asymmetry of the brain in dichotic listening', *Cortex*, vol. 3, p. 163.

KLUVER. H. (1958), 'The temporal lobe syndrome', in M. Baldwin and P. Bailey (eds.), *Temporal Lobe Epilepsy*, C. C. Thomas.

KOHN, B., and MYERS, R. E. (1969), 'Visual information and intermanual transfer of latchbox problem-solving in monkeys with commissures sectioned', *Exper. Neurol.*, vol. 23, p. 303.

KONORSKI, J. (1959), 'The physiological approach to the problem of recent memory', in J. F. Delafresnaye (ed.), *Brain Mechanisms and Learning*, Blackwell.

KRAL, V. A., and DUROST, H. B. (1953), 'A comparative study of the amnesic syndrome in various organic conditions', *Amer. J. Psychiat.*, vol. 110, p. 41.

LANSDELL, H. (1961), 'The effect of neurosurgery on a test of proverbs', *Amer. Psychol.*, vol. 16, p. 448.

LANSDELL, H. (1962), 'A sex difference in effect of temporal lobe neurosurgery on design preference', *Nature*, vol. 194, p. 582.

LASHLEY, W. S. (1929), *Brain Mechanisms and Intelligence*, University of Chicago Press.

LASHLEY, W. S. (1933), 'Integrative functions of the cerebral cortex', *Physiol. Rev.*, vol. 13, p. 1.

LEVINSON, F., and MEYER, V. (1965), 'Personality change in relation to psychiatric status following orbital cortex undercutting', *Brit. J. Psychiat.*, vol. 111, p. 207.

LEWIS, N. D. C., LANDIS, C., and KING, H. E. (1956), *Studies in Topectomy*, Grure and Strattion.

LOESER, J. D., and Alvord, E. C. (1968), 'Clinico-pathological correlations in agenesis of the corpus callosum', *Neurology*, vol. 18, p. 745.

LURIA, A. R. (1966), *Higher Cortical Functions in Man*, Tavistock.

LURIA, A. R., and HOMSKAYA, E. D. (1964), 'Disturbances in the regulative role of speech with frontal lobe lesions', in J. M. Warren and K. Akert (eds.), *The Frontal Granular Cortex and Behavior*, McGraw-Hill.

LURIA, A. R., NAYDIN, V. L., TSVETKOVA, T. S., and VINARSKAYA, E. N. (1969), 'Restoration of higher cortical function following local brain damage', in P. J. Vinken and G. W. Bruyn (eds.), *Handbook of Clinical Neurology*, vol. 3, North-Holland.

LURIA, A. R., SOKOLOV, E. N., and KLIMKOWSKI, M. (1967), 'Towards a neuro-dynamic analysis of memory disturbances with lesions of the left temporal lobe', *Neuropsychol.*, vol. 5, p. 1.

MCFIE, J., PIERCY, M. F., and ZANGWILL, O. L. (1951), 'The Rorschach test in obsessional neurosis with special reference to the effects of leucotomy', *Brit. J. Med. Psychol.*, vol. 24, p. 162.

McFie, J., and Zangwill, O. L. (1960), 'Visual constructive disabilities associated with lesions of the left cerebral hemisphere', *Brain*, vol. 83, p. 243.

McLeary, R. A., and Moore, R. Y. (1965), *Subcortical Mechanisms of Behaviour*, Basic Books.

Malmo, R. B. (1942), 'Interference factors in delayed response in monkeys after removal of the frontal lobes', *J. Neurophysiol.*, vol. 5, p. 295.

Malmo, R. B. (1948), 'Psychological aspects of frontal gyrectomy and frontal lobectomy in mental patients', *Res. Publ. Ass. Nerv. Ment. Dis.*, vol. 27, p. 537.

Malmo, R. B., and Amsel, A. (1948), 'Anxiety produced interference in serial rote learning with observations on rote learning after partial frontal lobectomy', *J. exp. Psychol.*, vol. 38, p. 440.

Meickle, T. H., and Sechzer, J. A. (1960), 'Interocular transfer of brightness discrimination in "split brain" cats', *Science*, vol. 132, p. 734.

Meier, M. J., and French, L. A. (1966), 'Longitudinal assessment of intellectual functioning following unilateral temporal lobectomy', *J. Clin. Psychol.*, vol. 22, p. 22.

Mettler, F. A. (1949), *Columbia-Greystone Associates – Selective Partial Ablations of the Frontal Cortex*, Routledge & Kegan Paul.

Mettler, F. A. (1952), *Columbia-Greystone Associates – Second Group. Psychosurgical Problems*, Routledge & Kegan Paul.

Meyer, V. (1959), 'Cognitive changes following temporal lobectomy for the relief of temporal lobe epilepsy', *Arch. Neurol. Psychiat.*, vol. 81, p. 299.

MEYER, V. (1960), 'Psychological effects of brain damage' in H. J. Eysenck (ed.), *Handbook of Abnormal Psychology*, Pitman.

MEYER, V., and JONES, H. G. (1957), 'Patterns of cognitive test performance as functions of the lateral localization of cerebral abnormalities in the temporal lobe', *J. ment. Sci.*, vol. 103, p. 758.

MEYER, V., and YATES, A. J. (1955), 'Intellectual changes following temporal lobectomy for psychomotor epilepsy', *J. Neurol. Neurosurg. Psychiat.*, vol. 18, p. 44.

MILLER, E. (1970), 'Simple and choice reaction time following severe head injury', *Cortex*, vol. 6, p. 121.

MILLER, E. (1971), 'Handedness and the pattern of human ability', *Brit. J. Psychol.*, vol. 62, p. 111.

MILNER, B. (1958), 'Psychological defects produced by temporal lobe excision', *Res. Publ. Ass. Nerv. Ment. Dis.*, vol. 36, p. 244.

MILNER, B. (1959), 'The memory defect in bilateral hippocampal lesions', *Psychiat. Res. Reports.*, vol. 11, p. 43.

MILNER, B. (1962), 'Laterality effects in audition' in V. B. Mountcastle (ed.), *Interhemispheric Relations and Cerebral Dominance*, Johns Hopkins Press.

MILNER, B. (1964), 'Some effects of frontal lobectomy in man', in J. M. Warren and K. Akert (eds.), *The Frontal Granular Cortex and Behavior*, McGraw-Hill.

MILNER, B. (1965), 'Visually-guided maze learning in man: effects of bilateral hippocompal, bilateral frontal and unilateral cerebral lesions', *Neuropsychol.*, vol. 3, p. 317.

MILNER, B. (1966), 'Amnesia following operation on the temporal lobes', in C. W. M. Whitty and O. L. Zangwill (eds), *Amnesia*, Butterworth.

MILNER, B., CORKIN, S., and TEUBER, H.-L. (1968), 'Further analysis of the hippocampal amnesic syndrome: fourteen year follow-up study of HM', *Neuropsychol.*, vol. 6, p. 215.

MILNER, B., TAYLOR, L., and SPERRY, R. W. (1970), 'Lateralized suppression of dichotically-presented digits after commissural section in man', *Science*, vol. 161, p. 184.

MISHKIN, M. (1954), 'Visual discrimination performance following partial ablations of the temporal lobe. II. Ventral surface vs. hippocampus', *J. comp. physiol. Psychol.*, vol. 47, p. 187.

MISHKIN, M. (1964), 'Perseveration of central sets after frontal lesions in monkeys', in J. M. Warren and K. Akert (eds.), *The Frontal Granular Cortex and Behavior*, McGraw-Hill.

MISHKIN, M., and PRIBRAM, K. H. (1954), 'Visual discrimination following partial ablations of the temporal lobe. II. Ventral vs. lateral', *J. comp. physiol. Psychol.*, vol. 47, p. 14.

MISHKIN, M. and PRIBRAM, K. H. (1955), 'Analysis of the effects of frontal lesions in monkeys: I. variations of delayed alternations', *J. comp. physiol. Psychol.*, vol. 48, p. 492.

MOFFETT, A. M., and ETTLINGER, G. (1970), 'Tactile discrimination performance in the monkey: the effect of unilateral posterior parietal lesions', *Cortex*, vol. 6, p. 47.

MYERS, R. E. (1955), 'Interocular transfer of pattern discrimination in cats following section of the crossed optic fibres', *J. comp. physiol. Psychol.*, vol. 48, p. 470.

MYERS, R. E. (1956), 'Function of corpus callosum in interocular transfer', *Brain*, vol. 79, p. 358.

MYERS, R. E. (1959a), 'Interhemispheric communication through corpus callosum: limitations under conditions of conflict', *J. comp. physiol. Psychol.*, vol. 52, p. 6.

MYERS, R. E. (1959b), 'Localization of function in the corpus callosum', *Arch. Neurol.*, vol. 1, p. 74.

MYERS, R. E., and HENSON, C. O. (1960), 'Role of the corpus callosum in transfer of tactuokinesthetic learning in chimpanzee', *Arch. Neurol.*, vol. 3, p. 404.

MYERS, R. E., and SPERRY, R. W. (1958), 'Interhemispheric communication through corpus callosum', *Arch. Neurol. Psychiat.*, vol. 80, p. 298.

MYERS, R. E., SPERRY, R. W., and MCCURDY, N. M. (1962), 'Neural mechanisms in visual guidance of limb movement', *Arch Neurol.*, vol. 7, p. 195.

ORBACH, J., and FANTZ, R. L. (1958), 'Differential effects of neocortical resections on overtrained and non-overtrained visual habits in monkeys', *J. comp. physiol. Psychol.*, vol. 51, p. 126.

ORBACH, J., MILNER, B., and RASMUSSEN, T. (1960), 'Learning and retention in monkeys after amygdala-hippocampus resections', *Arch. Neurol.*, vol. 3, p. 230.

OXBURY, J., and OXBURY, S. M. (1969), 'Effects of temporal lobectomy on the report of dichotically presented digits', *Cortex*, vol. 5, p. 3.

PASIK, T., PASIK, P., BATTERSBY, W. S., and BENDER, M. B. (1960), 'Factors influencing visual behavior of monkeys with bilateral temporal lobe lesions', *J. comp. Neurol.*, vol. 115, p. 89.

PAVLOV, I. P., (1927), *Conditioned Reflexes*, Oxford University Press.

PETRIE, A. (1949a), 'Preliminary report of changes after prefrontal leucotomy', *J. ment. Sci.*, vol. 95, p. 449.

PETRIE, A. (1949b), 'Personality changes after prefrontal leucotomy. Report two', *Brit. J. med. Psychol.*, vol. 22, p. 200.

PIERCY, M. (1964), 'The effects of cerebral lesions on intellectual function; a review of current research trends', *Brit. J. Psychiat.*, vol. 110, p. 310.

PIERCY, M., HECAEN, H., and de AJURIAGUERA, J. (1960), 'Constructional apraxia associated with unilateral cerebral lesions – left- and right-sided cases compared', *Brain*, vol. 83, p. 225.

PIERCY, M., and SMYTH, V.O.G. (1962), 'Right hemisphere dominance for certain non-verbal intellectual skills', *Brain*, vol. 85, p. 775.

PICKETT, J. M. (1952), 'Non-equipotential cortical functioning in maze learning', *Amer. J. Psychol.*, vol. 65, p. 177.

POPPEN, R. L., PRIBRAM, K. H., and ROBINSON, R. S. (1965), 'Effects of frontal lobotomy in man on the performance of a multiple choice task', *Exper. Neurol.*, vol. 2, p. 217.

PORTEUS, S. D. (1951), 'The Porteus Maze Test and psychosurgery', *Brit. J. med. Psychol.*, vol. 24, p. 132.

PRIBRAM, K. H. (1960), 'The intrinsic systems of the forebrain', in H. W. Magoun (ed.), *Handbook of Physiology. I. Neurophysiology*, vol. 2, American Physiological Society.

PRIBRAM, K. H., and MISHKIN, M. (1956), 'Analysis of the effects of frontal lesions in monkeys. III. Object Alternation', *J. comp. physiol. Psychol.*, vol. 49, p. 41.

PRIBRAM, K. H., and MISHKIN, M. (1958), 'Simultaneous and successive visual discriminations by monkeys with temporal lobe lesions', *J. comp. physiol. Psychol.*, vol. 48, p. 198.

REITAN, R. M. (1964), 'Psychological deficits resulting from cerebral lesions in man', in J. M. Warren and K. Akert (eds.), *The Frontal Granular Cortex and Behavior*, McGraw-Hill.

RIKLAN, M., and LEVITA, E. (1969), *Subcortical Correlates of Human Behavior*, Williams and Wilkins.

ROLLIN, A. R. (1955), 'Mass action effects in learning', *J. Psychol.*, vol. 39, p. 301.

ROSVOLD, H. E., and SZWARCBART, M. K. (1964), 'Neural structures involved in delayed response performance', in J. M. Warren and K. Akert (eds.), *The Frontal Granular Cortex and Behavior*, McGraw-Hill.

RUSSELL, J. R., and REITAN, R. M. (1955), 'Psychological abnormalities in agenesis of the corpus callosum', *J. nerv. ment. Dis.*, vol. 121, p. 205.

RYLANDER, G. (1951), 'Observations on mental changes after total lobotomy and after inferior lobotomy', *Acta Psychiat. et Neurol. Scand.*, Suppl. 60, p. 82.

SCHILDER, P., PASIK, T., and PASIK, P. (1968), 'Visual and tactual "go, no-go" discrimination in monkeys with temporal lobe lesions', *J. comp. physiol. Psychol.*, vol. 66, p. 811.

SCHRIER, A. M., and SPERRY, R. W. (1959), 'Visuomotor integration in split brain cats', *Science*, vol. 129, p. 1275.

SCOVILLE, W. B., and MILNER, B. (1957), 'Loss of recent memory after bilateral hippocampal lesions', *J. Neurol. Neurosurg. Psychiat.*, vol. 20, p. 11.

SEMMES, J. (1968), 'Hemispheric specialization: a possible clue to mechanism', *Neuropsychol.*, vol. 6, p. 11.

SEMMES, J., WEINSTEIN, S., GHENT, L., and TEUBER, H.-L. (1954), 'Performance on complex tactual tasks after brain injury in man: analysis by locus of lesion', *Amer. J. Psychol.*, vol. 67, p. 220.

SEMMES, J., WEINSTEIN, S., GHENT, L., and TEUBER, H.-L. (1955), 'Spatial orientation in man after cerebral injury: I. Analysis by locus of lesion', *J. Psychol.*, vol. 39, p. 227.

SEMMES, J., WEINSTEIN, S., GHENT, L., and TEUBER, H.-L. (1960), *Somatosensory Changes after Penetrating Brain Wounds in Man*, Harvard University Press.

SEMMES, J., WEINSTEIN, S., GHENT, L., and TEUBER, H.-L. (1963), 'Correlates of impaired orientation in personal and extrapersonal space', *Brain*, vol. 86, p. 747.

SHALLICE, T., and WARRINGTON, E. K. (1970), 'Independent functioning of verbal memory stores: a neuropsychological study', *Quart. J. exp. Psychol.*, vol. 22, p. 261.

SHANKWEILER, D. (1966), 'Effects of temporal lobe damage on perception of dichotically presented melodies', *J. comp. physiol. Psychol.*, vol. 62, p. 115.

SHAPIRO, M. B., BRIERLEY, J., SLATER, P., and BEECH, H. R. (1962), 'Experimental studies of a perceptual anomaly. VII. A new explanation', *J. ment. Sci.*, vol. 108, p. 655.

SMITH, A. (1960), 'Changes in Porteus maze scores of brain-operated schizophrenics after an eight year interval', *J. ment. Sci.*, vol. 106, p. 967.

SMITH, A. (1964), 'Changing effects of frontal lesions in man', *J. Neurol. Neurosurg. Psychiat.*, vol. 27, p. 511.

SMITH, A., and BURKLUND, C. W. (1966), 'Dominant hemispherectomy: preliminary report on neuropsychological sequelae', *Science*, vol. 153, p. 1280.

SPARKS, R., and GESCHWIND, N. (1968), 'Dichotic listening in man after section of the neocortical commissures', *Cortex*, vol. 4, p. 3.

SPERRY, R. W. (1964), 'The great cerebral commissure', *Scientific American*, vol. 211, p. 42.

SPERRY, R. W. (1968), 'Hemisphere deconnection and unity in conscious awareness', *Amer. Psychol.*, vol. 23, p. 723.

SPERRY, R. W., STAMM, J. S., and MINER, N. (1956), 'Relearning tests for interocular transfer following division of optic chiasma and corpus callosum in cats', *J. comp. physiol. Psychol.*, vol. 49, p. 529.

STAMM, J. S. (1969), 'Electrical stimulation of monkey's prefrontal cortex during delayed response performance', *J. comp. physiol. Psychol.*, vol. 67, p. 535.

STAMM, J. S., and SPERRY, R. W. (1957), 'Function of the corpus callosum in contralateral transfer of somesthetic discrimination in cats', *J. comp. physiol. Psychol.*, vol. 50, p. 138.

STEPIEN, L., CORDEAU, J. P., and RASMUSSEN, T. (1960), 'The effects of temporal lobe and hippocampal lesions on auditory and visual recent memory in monkeys', *Brain*, vol. 183, p. 470.

STEPIEN, L. S., and SIERPINSKI, S. (1960), 'The effect of focal lesions of the brain upon auditory and visual recent memory in man', *J. Neurol. Neurosurg. Psychiat.*, vol. 23, p. 334.

STEPIEN, L. S., and SIERPINSKI, S. (1964), 'Impairment of recent memory after temporal lesions in man', *Neuropsychol.*, vol. 2, p. 291.

SUBIRANA, A. (1958), 'Prognosis in aphasia in relation to cerebral dominance and handedness', *Brain*, vol. 81, p. 415.

SYMONDS, C. P. (1937), 'The assessment of symptoms following head injury', Guys Hospital Gazette, November, 1937, p. 1.

TAYLOR, D. C. (1969), 'Sexual behavior and temporal lobe epilepsy', *Arch. Neurol.*, vol. 21, p. 510.

TERZIAN, H. (1958), 'Observations on the clinical symptomatology of bilateral partial or total removal of the temporal lobes in man' in M. Baldwin and P. Bailey (eds.), *Temporal Lobe Epilepsy*, C. C. Thomas.

TEUBER, H.-L. (1955), 'Physiological Psychology', *Ann. Rev. Psychol.*, vol. 6, p. 267.

TEUBER, H.-L. (1964), 'The riddle of frontal lobe function in man', in J. M. Warren and K. Akert (eds.), *The Frontal Granular Cortex and Behavior*, McGraw-Hill.

TEUBER, H.-L., BATTERSBY, W. S., and BENDER, M. B. (1949), 'Changes in visual searching performance following cerebral lesions', *Amer. J. Physiol.*, vol. 159, p. 592.

TEUBER, H.-L., BATTERSBY, W. S., and BENDER, M. B. (1951), 'Performance of complex visual tasks after cerebral lesions', *J. rev. ment. Dis.*, vol. 184, p. 413.

TEUBER, H.-L., BATTERSBY, W. S., and BENDER, M. B. (1960), '*Visual Field Defects after Penetrating Missile Wounds of the Brain*, Harvard University Press.

TEUBER, H.-L., and BENDER, M. B. (1949), 'Alterations in pattern vision following trauma of occipital lobes in man', *J. Gen. Psychol.*, vol. 40, p. 37.

TREVARTHEN, C. B. (1962), 'Double visual learning in split-brain monkeys', *Science*, vol. 136, p. 258.

TREVARTHEN, C. B. (1965), 'Functional interactions between the cerebral hemispheres of the split-brain monkey', in G. Ettlinger (ed.), *Functions of the Corpus Callosum*, Churchill.

TREVARTHEN, C. B. (1969), '*Cerebral midline relations reflected in split-brain studies of the higher integrative functions*', paper presented to the Nineteenth International Congress of Psychology, London.

VAN WAGENEN, W. P., and HERREN, R. Y. (1940), 'Surgical division of commissural pathways in the corpus callosum; relation to spread of an epileptic attack', *Arch. Neurol. Psychiat.*, vol. 44, p. 740.

VIDOR, M. (1951), 'Personality changes following prefrontal leucotomy as reflected by the M.M.P.I. and the results of psychometric testing', *J. Ment. Sci.*, vol. 97, p. 159.

WADE, M. (1947), 'The effects of sedatives upon the delayed response in monkeys following removal of the prefrontal lobes', *J. Neurophysiol.*, vol. 10, p. 57.

WARREN, J. M., and AKERT, K. (eds.) (1964), *The Frontal Granular Cortex and Behavior*, McGraw-Hill.

WARRINGTON, E. K. (1962), 'The completion of visual forms across hemianopic field defects', *J. Neurol. Neurosurg. Psychiat.*, vol. 25, p. 208.

WARRINGTON, E. K. (1969), 'Constructional apraxia', in P. J. Vinken and G. W. Bruyn (eds.), *Handbook of Clinical Neurology*. Vol. 4, North-Holland.

WARRINGTON, E. K., JAMES, M., and KINSBOURNE, M. (1966), 'Drawing disability in relation to laterality of cerebral lesion', *Brain*, vol. 89, p. 53.

WARRINGTON, E. K., and WEISKRANTZ, L. (1970), 'Amnesic syndrome: consolidation or retrieval?', *Nature*, vol. 228, p. 628.

WATERHOUSE, I. K. (1957), 'Effects of prefrontal lobectomy on conditioned food and fear preferences in monkeys', *J. comp. physiol. Psychol.*, vol. 50, p. 81.

WEINGARTNER, H. (1968), 'Verbal learning in patients with temporal lobe lesions', *J. verb. Lear. verb. Behav.*, vol. 7, p. 520.

WEINSTEIN, S. (1954), 'Weight judgement in somesthesis after penetrating injury to brain', *J. comp. physiol. Psychol.*, vol. 47, p. 31.

WEINSTEIN, S. (1955a), 'Tactile size judgement after penetrating injury to the brain', *J. comp. physiol. Psychol.*, vol. 48, p. 106.

WEINSTEIN, S. (1955b), 'Time error in weight judgement after brain injury', *J. comp. physiol. Psychol.*, vol. 48, p. 203.

WEINSTEIN, S., SEMMES, J., GHENT, L., and TEUBER, H.-L. (1956), 'Spatial orientation in man after cerebral injury: analysis according to concomitant defects', *J. Psychol.*, vol. 42, p. 249.

WEINSTEIN, S., SEMMES, J., GHENT, L., and TEUBER, H.-L. (1958), 'Roughness discrimination after penetrating brain injury in man: analysis according to locus of lesion', *J. comp. physiol. Psychol.*, vol. 54, p. 269.

WEISKRANTZ, L. (1963), 'Contour discrimination in a young monkey with striate cortex ablation', *Neuropsychol.*, vol. 1, p. 145.

WEISKRANTZ, L. (1964), 'Impairment of learning and retention following experimental temporal lobe lesions', in M. A. B. Brazier (ed.), *Brain Function.* Vol. II. *RNA* and *Brain Function, Memory and Learning*, University of California Press.

WEISKRANTZ, L. (1968), *Analysis of Behavioural Change*, Harper & Row.

WEISKRANTZ, L., and COWEY, A. (1963), 'Striate cortex lesions and visual acuity of the rhesus monkey', *J. comp. physiol. Psychol.*, vol. 56, p. 225.

WEISKRANTZ, L., MIHAILOVIĆ, J., and GROSS, C. G. (1962), 'Effects of stimulation of frontal cortex and hippocampus on behaviour of the monkey', *Brain*, vol. 85, p. 487.

WEISKRANTZ, L., and WILSON, W. A. (1958), 'The effect of ventral rhinencephalic lesions on avoidance thresholds in monkeys', *J. comp. physiol. Psychol.*, vol. 51, p. 167.

WICKELGREN, W. A. (1968), 'Sparing of short-term memory in an amnesic patient: implications for strength theory of memory', *Neuropsychol.*, vol. 6, p. 235.

WILLIAMS, M. (1970), *Brain Damage and the Mind*, Penguin.

WILSON, M. (1957), 'Effects of circumscribed cortical lesions upon somesthetic and visual discrimination in the monkey', *J. comp. physiol. Psychol.*, vol. 50, p. 630.

WILSON, M., STAMM, J. A., and PRIBRAM, K. H. (1960), 'Deficits in roughness discrimination after posterior parietal lesions in monkeys', *J. comp. physiol. Psychol.*, vol. 53, p. 535.

WYKE, M. (1966), 'Postural arm drift associated with brain lesions in man', *Arch. Neurol.*, vol. 15, p. 329.

WYKE, M., and ETTLINGER, G. (1961), 'Efficiency of recognition in right and left visual fields: its relation to the phenomenon of visual extinction', *Arch. Neurol.*, vol. 5, p. 659.

ZANGWILL, O. L. (1960), *Cerebral Dominance and its Relation to Psychological Function*, Oliver & Boyd.

Index

Brain Damage and the Mind

Dr Moyra Williams

The effects of brain damage provide valuable information about the working of the healthy mind and also give clues to further progress in the clinical field. Dr Williams' survey presents this information clearly and usefully under the familiar categories of consciousness and mood, memory, perception, motor skill and verbal expression, and intelligence and personality. An interesting conclusion offers a tentative model of mental activity.

Dr Moyra Williams is the principal clinical psychologist, Department of Psychiatry, Addenbrooke's Hospital, Cambridge.

Behaviour Therapy in Clinical Psychiatry

This book is a thorough, balanced account of the theory, practice and effectiveness of behaviour therapy. This form of treatment, derived from experimental psychology, plays a growing role in the treatment of many disorders, such as anxiety, alcoholism, sexual deviations, stammering, tics and enuresis. Its techniques have at times also been successfully employed in psychoses, psychosomatic disorders, obsessional neuroses and childhood behaviour disorders.

After a brief introduction to psychiatric disorders for readers unfamiliar with clinical psychiatry, chapter 2 gives a full account of the relevant theories of conditioning and learning, and chapter 3 considers how well experimental psychology can account for psychiatric disorders. Chapter 4 reviews the main methods of treatment in behaviour therapy such as desensitization, aversion therapy, 'flooding' or implosive therapy, and operant conditioning, while chapter 5 looks very carefully at the empirical evidence for the effectiveness of these methods. After two chapters that offer a wide-ranging view of current research, chapter 8 confronts the practical world of the clinic – the problems that arise in the selection of patients, selection of symptoms to be treated, method of treatment, selection of therapist, and in the conduct of treatment. 'An attempt is made', the authors explain, 'to discuss these topics in a constructive manner based on our experience with a variety of behaviour therapy methods employed in the treatment of 150 patients, the majority of whom were suffering from psycho-neurotic disorders with a preponderance of phobic anxiety states.'

A short conclusion looks to the prospects of treatment and research in behaviour therapy units.

This text should be of interest to those already engaged in clinical practice or research and those undergoing training who may choose to enter this field. It should therefore be of value to those training or practising in clinical psychology, psychiatry, psychiatric social work and occupational therapy.

'This concise and readable book fills a long-felt need.'
Lancet

Victor Meyer is Reader in Clinical Psychology, Academic Department of Psychiatry, Middlesex Hospital Medical School.

Edward S. Chesser is Nuffield Fellow and Honorary Lecturer in Psychiatry, Middlesex Hospital Medical School.

Penguin Science of Behaviour

Assessment in Clinical Psychology
C. E. Gathercole

Basic Statistics in Behavioural Research
A. E. Maxwell

Beginnings of Modern Psychology
W. M. O'Neil

Brain Damage and the Mind
Moyra Williams

The Development of Behaviour
W. Mary Woodward

Disorders of Memory and Learning
George A. Talland

Feedback and Human Behaviour
John Annett

The Growth of Sociability
H. R. Schaffer

Interpersonal Perception
Mark Cook

An Introduction to Social Psychiatry
Ransom J. Arthur

Listening and Attention
Neville Moray

Mathematical Models in Psychology
Frank Restle

On the Experience of Time
Robert E. Ornstein

Pathology of Attention
Andrew McGhie

Pattern Recognition
D. W. J. Corcoran

Personal Relationships in Psychological Disorders
Gordon R. Lowe

Psychometric Assessment of the Individual Child
R. Douglass Savage

Schools and Socialization
A. Morrison and D. McIntyre

Socialization
Kurt Danziger

Small Group Psychotherapy
Edited by Henry Walton

The Study of Twins
Peter Mittler

Teachers and Teaching
A. Morrison and D. McIntyre

Vigilance and Attention
Jane F. Mackworth

Vigilance and Habituation
Jane F. Mackworth